SITUATION REPORTS ON THE EMOTIONAL EQUIPOISE

SITUATION REPORTS ON THE EMOTIONAL EQUIPOISE

Collected Poems 1959-2006

Brewster Chamberlin

Copyright © 2007 by Brewster Chamberlin.

ISBN: Softcover   978-1-4257-7950-4

All rights reserved. No part of this book may be reproduced or transmitted in any form or by any means, electronic or mechanical, including photocopying, recording, or by any information storage and retrieval system, without permission in writing from the copyright owner.

This book was printed in the United States of America.

To order additional copies of this book, contact:
Xlibris Corporation
1-888-795-4274
www.Xlibris.com
Orders@Xlibris.com
40872

CONTENTS

A Vision	23
Christmas in the Village	24
Sonny Rollins	25
For a Lover Early in the Game	26
Sadness—for Spring	27
Autumn	28
Dave Brubeck	29
Elegy for a Pruned Bud	30
Beginning	32
Paul Desmond	34
The Specter	35
Exile	36
The Paupers	37
Incident	38
Pop Song	39
Aftermath	40
Notations	41
Lennie Tristano	42
The Quiet	43
Bourgeois Parents' 1954 Dilemma	44
Mid-Indian Summer	45
For Van Gogh	46
Unvanquished	47
Winter's Tale	48
Sea Glimpse	49
November Day—Heidelberg 1961	50
Death of a Man	52
Piano Player	53
A Poet's Haiku	54
Barroom Talk	55
On the Death of W. H. Auden	56
On Reading Cavafy in 1976	57

Song for the Gone Poets	58
Shorts	60
The Baroque Takeover	61
Poet's Salvation	62
On Remembering Jones Beach	63
Wide Horizons	64
I laid the floor . . .	65
Sunday on Columbia Road	66
Windows	67
Doors	68
Confusion	69
Nice Times	70
Quiet Nights	71
Spilled Wine Blues	72
The Heart's Lamb Chops	73
Runny Noses	74
March Musings	75
Sundays at Home	76
No Photograph	77
Gift Horses	78
In the Tombs	79
Bach: Solo Cello	80
You looked so lovely . . .	81
Two Poems in Memory of Frank O'Hara	82
Rachel of the Skyscraper	83
The Color of Paradise	84
Fear and Loathing	85
The Farouk Epic	86
O Yeats!	87
Questions	88
On Sitting at a Gas Station	89
A Metaphysical Justification	90
The Plain Truth and a True Fact	91
Dangerous Acts	92
Dream of an Unknown Beach in Paradise	93
Ecology	94
Goodbye-Hello/Existential Angst	95
Paradise Reviewed	96
Cavafy's Dream	97

Changes	98
Beginnings	100
Airports play games . . .	101
Poem Written in the Cold	102
Dylan Thomas Remembered on a Bus in Vermont	103
Cul de sac	104
Premonition	105
A Message in the German	106
Missed Connections	107
"Do you have to leave?"	108
Two Early Spring Poems	109
Wages of Sin	110
Lynn-Marie Traveling	111
Oh distant lady . . .	112
Untermeyer's Beddoes Ash	114
Heavy Wind	115
Ikonology	116
Rites	117
Sun Dance	118
At the Pier	119
On the Graylight Beach	121
The Addy Sea I	122
One Summer at Bethany Beach	123
In the Torpedo Factory	125
TV	126
On Leaving from Red Hook	127
Before the War	129
Friday Afternoon	130
The Porch	131
The Garden Café	132
Autumn Turns to Winter Too Swiftly	133
Evening Rushes	134
Such as We	135
An Event	136
Where to Go	137
On the Avenue	138
Love Song	139
Song	141
The Last Race	142

Gypsy Music 143
The Attic..144
Taken Out...145
Interregnum 146
Spanish Night 147
Hochbegabte Schweinerei...148
Chicago Layover..149
Empty Suit or Paul Newman's Chica OD'd in the South Bronx Streets 150
The Wink 151
Lines for Lynn-Marie One Afternoon..152
A Criminal Act..153
Bethany Beach 1980..154
The Month of May 155
An Imagined Return 156
Saloon..157
Captain Harry...158
The Addy Sea II 159
For Ernst Toller in Memoriam..160
An Objective Day..161
On Awakening 162
At the Beach..163
The Writer in Mississippi 164
Variations on a Theme 165
Aliens in Paradise 166
Intimations of Another World...167
Quest 168
Harry Lime 169
The Saving Grace 170
The Fall..171
The Young Professor...172
The Solution 173
At the Shore 174
March 26 175
Manhattan Melody 176
The Audience..177
On the Corner of 4th Street & 6th Avenue 178
Sin and Redemption...179
The Addy Sea III 180
Morning...181

The New Projector	182
The Marriage Season	183
E pluribus unum	184
Apocalypse in Barcelona	185
The Athens Hilton	186
Delphi	187
Ruins at Delphi	188
Cretan Moon	189
Daughter's Lament on Missing Her Bottle	190
The New Poet	191
Reflection at Mid-Point	192
Ten Poses	193
For Romy Schneider	195
Music and the Beast	196
Moving On	197
Blind Luck	198
In the Garrigue	199
Beginning in Provence	200
On Hearing Monk in Provence	201
To the Rombauers	202
First Mistral	203
Winter Sounds	204
In the Mistral	205
Avignon 1983	206
Chez moi	207
Le sang du poète	208
Épisode quotidian chez Mme Moure	209
Tavel Morning	210
At the Edge: The Tune Inn	211
High Summer in Provence	212
The Fishermen and the Poets	214
Summation	215
Walls	216
Last Train Out	217
Memorials	218
Three Sisters	219
The Wrong Target	220
Vincent et Pablo	221
Washington December	222

Sick Days 223
After the Fog 224
The Lost Lady 225
Baths and Showers 226
Brown Bag 227
Bookshelves Pleasures 228
Where I Live 229
Cum grano salis 230
August 1, 1989 231
Winter 1989 232
The New Criticism 233
On the Death in Paris of Samuel Beckett on December 22, 1989 234
Me and Julie Maigret 235
Knowledge Hunger 236
Friendly Fire 237
On Visiting the Petrarch Museum At the Fontaine de la Vaucluse 238
The Absolute Point of it All 239
Weekend in Toulouse 240
Johnny Mack Brown Spends a Night in Tunisia 242
The Future of the Race 243
Departures 244
An Act of Love 245
Old Man's Day Dreams 246
Notions of the Young Joyce 247
Our Daily Bread 248
Never-Never Land 249
Airborne 250
Yoplait Meets Dannon or Creative Lit-Crit Unveiled 251
Unemployment Blues 253
The Indigent 254
The Shadow's Message 255
Corfu Nights 256
On the Afterdeck at Louie's 257
Thinking of Durrell in Key West 258
The Watchtower 259
B-Girls on a Roll 260
Key West Gecko Serenade 261
Sunrise in Key West 263
Mausoleum for a Dead Writer 264

At the Cemetery in Key West 265
Tropical Afternoon 266
The Offering 267
Rivers of Nostalgia/Oceans of Kitsch 268
Diversion 269
Love's Poison 270
Along the Liston, Corfu 271
The Place to Go 273
Scrambled Paradise 274
In Durrell's Footsteps 275
Soliloquy 276
Ron Died 277
The Corfu Event 278

For

Maddalena DeMaria
the first muse
who bore the burden

and

Lynn-Marie Smith
the final muse
who bears it now forever

Listen, pal, forget what they told you
at school. Poetry's for anybody, at
any time, anywhere. All you gotta do
is *read* it, mon. See?

> —Eden the Perfect Bartender to a
> despairing undergraduate at
> The Edge Bar, Dorset, Vermont in
> the Summer of 1943.

Preface

You, The Reader, are about to take a journey covering almost half a century and you are owed some brief explanation about the fragmented chronology of the poems in this volume. The text below may provide such without, it is hoped, unduly imposing on your patience. Ventures such as these are inevitably concerned with autobiography, but this aspect of these introductory words has been kept to a minimum.

Following the example of Cavafy and so many others in the tradition of private printing, these verses now, long after their creation, finally see the light of the published page, with only minor adjustments in some cases to correct a gross infelicity or stupidity where the poem could be even rescued from the right-handed author's youthful gaucherie. An author, it must be admitted, who firmly believed, then, he would become an artist of the English language, and spend the rest of his life writing poems, novels, stories, depending upon the tender mercies of Fate and the book-buying public to afford him the opportunity to pay the rent and the grocer's invoices. Fate, at least, took care of the opportunity: one got a job that paid the bills. The writing had to be done at night and on weekends. But one did write: mainly academic scholarship, and administrative memoranda and program progress reports, but not poems, novels and stories, not during the day. Some can work steadily under these conditions, some cannot.

The earlier poems are clearly of their time, influenced by poets straining for communion with a transcendent idea in praxis, poets with whom one associated to one extent or another or at least read and listened to with attention: Kenneth Rexroth, Allan Ginsberg, Gregory Corso, Jack Mitchell, Ted Joans—all of whom should have streets named after them in American cities.

The sparseness of poems between 1961 and 1975 is due in good part to that unavoidable necessity mentioned above, years of work during the day and formal education at night, full time graduate work in the misguided belief that this would be the ticket to the grand American theater of Academia. One spent eight of those years in Europe, mainly in Germany, working and living hard, with little time for writing poems or anything else except academic texts on the cinema and European history.

One theory of literary creation posits that most forms of literature, but most particularly poetry, are created during periods in which the writer experiences personal upheaval, a volatile combining of the extremes of joy and pain, at a level of intensity which demands a creative outlet in order that the writer survives emotionally and psychologically, in order that some sense be made of the swooping shifts of emotion in a hurly-burly of instability and erratic behavior. During the years 1978-1980 one struggled with this potentially destructive, if banal, pattern. Could one call this period "the dark night of the soul"? That would, of course, satisfy a certain nostalgia for the Faustian situation beloved by Romantics, but this would not be a completely accurate description of one's own situation. Nonetheless, the ratcheting tremors rattled the foundations of one's existence with sufficient savagery to require something to hold on to in that slippery world—poetry seemed to allow the possibility of organizing the turbulence that so terrifyingly staggered one's life at the time.

The years following 1980 allowed varying periods of creativity quite different from previous times. This is reflected in a return to prose as the main form of expression, which one continued to use productively, if irregularly, given the continuing necessity to ensure that the holes in the roof are patched and that the digestive system has something to digest, though the rent by now has become mortgage payments. A year (1982-83) spent in the Provençal village of Tavel, close to Avignon, writing, painting and enjoying the finest rosé wine in France, or anywhere else for that matter, is memorialized in the poems written there, when one was freed briefly from the necessity to earn the grocery money—a situation unrepeated until the autumn of 2001 when Lynn-Marie and I moved to Key West and a life devoted, in my case, to writing (prose mostly) almost full time, in a place where there is no winter and the Cuban coffee wakes you in the morning with a bang.

I have made use of the author's prerogative when assembling collected works: this means I have made some revisions to certain older poems I thought would enhance the value and quality of those poems and have indicated which ones they are by adding the year 2006 to their date of composition.

Avignon 1993—Key West 2007

Note

"Exile" was previously printed in the journal *Deus Loci*, NS4 (1995-96). "High Summer in Provence," "The Fishermen and the Poets," "At the Edge: The Tune Inn," "Portaria," "Épisode quotidian chez Mme Moure," and "Thinking of Durrell in Key West" were previously printed in *Mediterranean Sketches* (Vineyard Press, 2005) and "Soliloquy," "The Watchtower," "The Shadow's Message," Along the Liston, Corfu," "Sunrise in Key West," Mausoleum for a Dead Writer," "The Island Question," "Key West Gecko Serenade," "The Indigent," "At the Cemetery in Key West," On the Afterdeck at Louie's," "In Durrell's Footsteps," "Tropical Afternoon," "B-Girls on a Roll," and "Love's Poison" previously appeared in *Love's Poison and Other Poems 2000-2005* (privately printed illustrated limited edition, Key West, 2006).

A Vision

A pebble strikes a pool
The lamb becomes the Tiger
The blank blanched wall of white anger
Looms with gigantic intensity
Before the bronzelidded eyes of night
Screaming helplessly against the light.

Spring 1959

Christmas in the Village

For Bob Ford, who was there

Christmas in the Village
Empty streets pregnant
With the crystal stillness of icicles
The cold seems to press in his warmth
As the walker alone crosses the square
In search of nothing
Listening to the brittle air's
Crackling steely conversation
Even the Charles Street garages
Seem to say hello as he walks by
Breath steaming light and airy
The shuttered shops hold promises
And the open unaffordable restaurants
Glow inside with gay open fires
His heels ring in the quiet
His steps point toward nowhere
Aimlessly drifting about almost smiling
Ending in a small coffee shop
Where the young waitress smiled
Serving coffee and donuts for dinner.

1959/1993

Sonny Rollins

Earlier Bird's reincarnation
Now sounding his own story
He strides manynoted across the scenery:
Roaring, blasting strident horn
Hard grinding sympathetic soul

The cowboy colossus gallops on
Into the horn-hung dark night.
The preacher on his up altar
Talking his congregation truth.
A huge eagle that can change to swan

Enfolds with his wings the anger
Of his generation's madness,
And from his horn clear it overflows
Like the onslaught of a hundred tons
Of explosion released tidal wave,

Spreading over and enveloping
Who know enough to listen,
To that prophetic soul who may not
Know exactly where he's going
But moves on ahead regardless, unafraid.

1959

For a Lover Early in the Game

The moon rides the crest of the

silvery transparent apparitions

        and floats

its radiance, brilliantly, tenderly

enfolding the night in its

        invisible arms.

And this, not even the whisper

of the beginning of you.

        1959

Sadness—for Spring

In the breezy stillness of March,
   When life is cyclically beginning,
   for the hundredth millionth time,
   And joy flows through every leaf and twig,
   Why do I feel a little emptiness
      and wonderingly incomplete?

   Youth must be the answer,
   I can think of no other;
      yes, my youth is surely the reason,
   In the Spring of joy and rejoicing,
   For this terrible vagueness of being.

   But look, I tell myself,
   One is not youthful long,
      soon age creeps over the hill
   And then the Spring months of gladness
   Will give to you the same thoughts and feelings
      I see and hear
            in leaves
                   and twigs
   Around me now.

                            1959

Autumn

For Maddalena

The leaves turn brown
And fall from their high places,
Slipping softly to the ground,
Covering the flowers' grinning faces.

Then to ashes, then to dust,
All coming under the power
Of Winter's great lust.
And the laughing flower

Stifled, the running brook in halter;
The sounds of summer no longer heard.
Gentle stillness on a white alter
And across the sun sings the last Spring bird.

And again the blazing white sun
Becomes a round black ball.
"Where is he gone, my son, my son?"
And Winter is here, after the Fall.

Spring 1959

Dave Brubeck

Balconies rocking with
Two fisted unheard of
Polytonality.
Put down for
Coming down,
Swinging on evergreens
Through ivyed halls,
Pouring over Schönberg,
Pouring out Miles,
He gives his own:
Too weighty dragging shoes
Suddenly stopped driving
And began skipping
Lightly down his lane.
Like a baby's first words
Weighted hands rock
Ponderously
Across the empty slate,
Singing his own story
In his own sweet way.

1959

Elegy for a Pruned Bud

I got fingers
    man
I know
    I've got fingers.
Why? Dunno.
To play, to blow—kblang!
    on black and white no time keys
Entrance to the soul.

(Fastest lefthanded Cherokee to you Art)

I had it then—time ago
    but man
I still might have it—
    there's all the other
    withered
    decaying
    lost.

    Me?
        Hell it's other people.
    Like it's personal
        terrifying personal
    And but done man
    IN A GLASS WALLED ROOM
    man
        without silence
        (clinkle clangkle yessir scotch
        gin and tonic)
    Tell me someone
        yell
        scream
        reach me!

    How do you make it?

                               1959

Beginning

I SEE THE END OF THE WORLD AS WE KNOW IT.

I HAVE A VISION OF BLAKIAN HORROR
of the world in massed milling confusion
and endless destruction until nothing remains
except the voice of man
like an ant in a jungle of elephants.

I SEE THE END OF THE WORLD
where love only exists
in hot feverish embraces,
where faith is in the mentality of apes,
where man is confessed unto man
and not God, whom he can never see
(only the black-robed figure representing life).

I SEE ONLY MAN IN INNOCENCE ENDURING
through love which is not understanding
but truth, reality, and the ultimate.
The muck crawling groveling is doomed
and man will stand proudly,
face and heart uplifted, soul soaring,
and look into the face of the desolate isolation
which is not eternity.

MAN COMES OF AGE
only when his manliness is destroyed
and his humanity is redeemed,
coming only from within himself
when he is ready and capable.

HE IS NOT
    now,
but he will be
when this vision comes to pass,
and the evil that is man now,
without love and unable to trust,
is at last destroyed
in a day of judgment that no one expects.

THE ANT WILL SPEAK, AND BE HEARD,
and will be immortal.

1959

Paul Desmond

A soft silvery thread
Weaving lyrics in and out
Of ominous surge of chords.

Tension tight, timeless note
Follows quick thought note.

Sometimes reality
A clearer mirror
Of you and me and them.

Lightly with the strength
Of trees in a breeze,
The horn speaks, whispers
Out the song of himself.

1959/1993

The Specter

One day while dozing on a hillside
I saw through the tides of sleep.
Saw things I thought I'd never see again—

>children playing in the woods next door
>a birthday celebration—seven candled cake
>mistakes made once—sometimes more
>a boy and a girl swinging in a meadow
>>innocent of the world
>schoolboys becoming college men
>>first pulling little girls' hair
>>then caressing it
>marriage in a small pale church
>birth in a large white hospital
>a short line of black cars
>>lights on in daylight . . .

Then a birdsong awakened me
and I knew I would never see them again
except once more
regretfully.

January 1960

Exile

For Lawrence Durrell
(The new poet of the city)

And so we came back to the city
Looking at reminders of old
To trigger the works of memory,
Attempting to recover lost images
Forgotten in the choked halls of time;
Searching out hidden remembrances
Foundering in the dark crevices of the mind;
Soon we discovered, with a great sense of loss,
That while the forms were there, the city,
The content was gone, the part of us
That we had left there.
And we knew finally, we had left nothing
There, but had taken all with us,
And lost it with experience,
To return again only in dreams
When we are far away.

July 1960

The Paupers

So one minute you're Cleopatra,
Another Juliet,
Another Isolde;
But you don't act like any of them
When life comes to face us.

We hide behind masks of rubber
When love smiles upon us, our
Answer is but a hesitant half-smile.

How can I be Tristan, or any one,
In this suffocating contraption?

Our love blazes in the afternoon
in whispers behind drawn shades.

August 1960

Incident

They were taking him home by train
    in a long wooden black box
    that smelled strangely
and they were playing cards in the mail car
    and not noticing or paying any attention
    at all to the long black box that held him.
Then he rose up out of the box and looked at them
    but they didn't see him for the cards
    except one small insect in the corner
    who saw him shake his head, and knew.

                                                   1960

Pop Song

For Johnnie Ray

The snow falls gently to the ground
    softly as a caress,
Covers the embryonic shoots that
    thrust through the earth's crust.

Saddened hearts wind-whipped
    around empty corners
Down barren city streets
    lie unmolested melting into the curb.

Couples forced inside themselves
    by the ironic whiteness descending,
Parted from the sanctuary of each other:
    there's snow in lovers' lane.

1960/1993

Aftermath

Finished again
rolled off into another sweaty rooting sleep
satisfaction snores

But you
unfinished
something missing from the beginning

The bare walls look greyer
dingy blinds cut out the moonlight
leftover taste all over

Quicksilver streak of nausea
slices through the fading climax thrill

Get up
trail a thin fingerline
through yesterday's dust on the nightstand

Look at the twisted yellow sheets
marks of combat
the battle is done
the war goes on

Weep empty.

1960

Notations

New England Winter

a string quintet

playing dry brittle music

on a snowy afternoon

snowflakes snap in the cold air.

                                                        1960

Lennie Tristano

Alone in darkness
    not looking for a light outside
    but introspective searching.

Iconoclastic monk
    solitude surrounding
    always new designs

Given out seemingly indifferent
    but beneath the outer freeze
    writhes lonely fire and spirit.

Cold intellectual sound some hear
    going no deeper than funk and flesh
    not getting it at all

The tumult of searing outrage
    the vital pulsing organism
    barely contained by a biting mind

Alone in darkness
    looking for its own blinding light
    of new frontiers and sounds.

1960/1993

The Quiet

The quiet, the quiet

finely spun cobwebs creeping over my ears

around my brain, walling me in

I hear the quiet creaking through the rooms

coming closer and nearer

old as time, new as my next silent breath

I see it as fog seeps in the cracks

under the door, along the window panes

slowly, out of the east

it brings sleep, long and pale

a vague vanishing face behind a clouded window

upon me, at last, I succumb to its embrace.

19.VI.1961

Bourgeois Parents' 1954 Dilemma

How to explain

in one afternoon

the concept of ethics

to a hotrod loon?

1961

Mid-Indian Summer

After Summer's cool dimness
in Wade's store's shadowy rooms—
Pigeon Cove's multi-colored sails
on the bluegreen waters,
a rainbow of small sea birds
against the pale grey sky.

Then it was Autumn
the shadows at the foot of
the iron Gloucester fisherman
shrank into themselves—
the water colder, the cement harder
the wharf fishstink subsided midtown.

Young Ahabs dimly eye school doors
as they pass toward one last voyage.

1961/1993

For Van Gogh

Vincent, Vincent
You lovely mad soul,
absinthe soaked sunworshiper.
The sun was your undoing
and your key to eternity.

O mortal Icarus, the fiery eye
blazes down upon your tender wings
flapping for infinity.

Vincent, I cry to you from my vision:
Compadre!
The Arles sun will never shine so bright.

The manifestation of your soul
overwhelms my eyes and I am blinded
so I can finally see.

1961/1993

Unvanquished

They came at me over the crest of the hill:
    hundreds of them, obstinately pouring forth,
Their minute brains roaring with stifled life
    in craniums much too small for them,
Signaling each other silently, seemingly leaderless
    and chaotic in form and plan,
But following a terrible pattern of ever-expanding
    dimensions fearful to contemplate.
They came down on the hill deliberately
    with courage in numbers:
Even in thousands they're small and soft-shelled.
    I fought back with fire and water,
Brooms and feet until, because I was a giant,
    I had driven them back up the hill
And down the other side;
    again I could rest, nervously, for I knew
They would be back once more, this time
    more cautiously, with more knowledge
Of the enemy, and more hardened
    in their diabolical plan:
To conquer the world and rule as masters.
    Those ants, they'll be back, I know it.
Those ants, those damned damned ants.

                                            10.IV.1961

Winter's Tale

The day begins gray and empty
Except for the brittle stillness
Creeping slowly out of the East
To subdue the chirping sounds of the small bird
Keeping warm in a secluded thicket off the road
Soon to be strangled by thundering automobiles.

But now in the early morning silence
Mist rolls creaking over the dewshrouded landscape
And before the beginning sounds of people are heard
A small child presses her face against the cold
Enclosing transparent pane and looking out on the
World her sleepy face is distorted with silent horror
And she runs terrified back to bed
Pulls the covers over her head and shivers.

1961

Sea Glimpse

For Larry Adamo

Protean catchall
Like the multilevel mind of man
Paradox of whirlpools and smooth surfaces
Calm clear mild surface
Turbulent tortured bottom
Foamgrown in the sloughs
Crestharvested chunks windblown
Piledriver driven against aged rocks
Thunderous self-ovation
In appreciation of its own terrible beauty
But soft slow undulating ripples
Peaceful ripples lolling whispering to themselves
Windcaressed.

1961

November Day—Heidelberg 1961

For Angela

Look for me along the sunny Neckar
That's where I'll be
Baking the cold out of my soul,
Along the unloved day
Racing away from the anesthetic night.
Softly, with furry seductive sadness,
Seeking the last day's warmth.

Look for me along the flowing Neckar
That's where I'll be
Straightening the twisted heart
That beats straining against my chest,
Gift-given it gives its gift
And once again I rejoice and suffer
All the love you have to offer.

Look for me along the calming Neckar
That's where I'll be
Singing songs of love and death:
Beguiling ballads the hours long,
Time to kill with troubadour's rhymes
Bury with lyrics of the heart
Pray over with the artifice of art.

Look for me along the gentle Neckar
That's where I'll be
Across the Alte Brücke in the day's
Weary tearscarred light.
Come armed in search of me,
Alone I'm suicidal
(the watery whispering grave)
But come in search of me
Or I'll never find you.

Death of a Man

Wind careens around the corner keening,
Speeds down the street in stiff short gusts
Jerking wastepaper upwards and sideways.
The domed bleakgrey sky
Leers down at the smashed wine bottles,
Waiting for the bent greasestained creature
Ragged on the corner, eyes shifting, also waiting,
The wind flaying his caked skin too numb to shiver.
Finally, crab-like, infinitely slow he moves painfully,
Two, three steps, closer and closer,
The wind screaming at him in the gathering darkness.
His scabbed prehensile claw reaches out,
He begins to bend forward, stumbles, falls.
The wind tears at the heaped bundle of clothing
And dashes on down the street
Keening into the darkness.

14.XI.1961
Heidelberg

Piano Player

> Song is the simple rhythmic
> liberation of an emotion.
> -James Joyce: *Stephen Hero*

To play, to play,
To play my life away.
It's been so long: endless chunks of time,
Since my spread fingers have
Careened, plucked, pounded
These keys on which I recreate my life.

Ah, sweet expression of all passion,
From treble to bass, arpeggios
Running away with my hands following.
Release of all daydreams
At once vapors of unconsciousness
And noted reality.

To feel the guts of the piano
      Roll and groan to the touch
      Waltz and skitter at will
      Improvised blues of my life
      Wailed across the room against the wall.

To play, to play.
It's been so long since I've
Pressed the keys to my soul.

1962, Heidelberg

A Poet's Haiku

A poem

a day

keeps the

shrink away.

April, 1975

Barroom Talk

One loudmouth said

    This poor bastard thinks he's a poet.

The chorus swiftly answered

    Drown him before it's too late.

                            June 1976

On the Death of W. H. Auden

Finally snuffled the last mucous bit
in a comfy bourgeois Wiener hotel;
at last let loose from the small pains
which filled the last years' weary days.
But also ambiguously freed from the dry
American martini taste in provincial Kirchstetten
    (now inevitably to become a shrine,
    to the joy of the locals—
    but must Chester move?)
The quickening of joy and ecstasy at
completing a unique phrase or
daily crossword puzzle—finished now
along with the pain.
But enough was enough, nicht wahr?
The need for vespers has long since
whitewashed the heart if not the mind:
the solutions now came in black and white
no longer a youthful red.
The end is usually nasty and a bore.
One hopes this end in the Flickenstrasse
in the bosom of the lamb and Etagemädchen
was fast and violent, the final spasm.

No longer worried about dirty fingernails,
he is surely still revising.

                                      1976

On Reading Cavafy in 1976

What is this inert aura
suffusing the pages?
The odor of dry faded lilacs
stale Egyptian cigarettes
ambiguous sensuousness of Levantine rooms.

What can these aromas—
drifting languorously up behind
those pleading, intelligent words—
mean in this age
except to reinforce their own anachronism
in our distracted longing for the past?

June 1976

Song for the Gone Poets

When the blasted heath
becomes the gas ovens
we either forget or
throw away our pens.
        —The broken house poet
        of The Edge Bar, Mid—
        20th Century

And here's to them what can roll their eyes
    like they rolls their R's.
Loutish, besotted brutes at their wine and poems
They flushed the quail like Prufrock his toilet.
For them no fields of amaranth and asphodel,
For them the vernal shires in the solstice sun
And the tunnels of the city in the snow.

But now, in their ever constricting vistas
    they utter no bellows and roars
No more, no more the smoke rasped gurgle
    rising to a bawling clamor.

Now we've but the limpid curlicues of self-abuse
Raised to epigone, tragedy and boredom.

But here's to them what could drown
    the gaping gullet of Ireland.
Sorry that they've gone because
The imaginations of Caligula and Heliogabalus
    have no space here in Middletown
Where the demons of the East are exorcised
    in 24 frames per second.

Aye, there's no blackspot possible here.
It's all in Madame Tussaud—
    step right up
    and take a gander . . .

June 1976

Shorts

I.
The rain in the clouds
is reaching
the top of a mountain
that is not there.

II.
On Waiting to See Two Kurasowa Films

The orient is not so
much impenetrable
as semantically exotic.
A labyrinth with
too many exits.

III.
Some patterns
traces of flower forms
amidst congested industrial
stenches.
The soul struggling
to maintain itself.

IV.
Pity the poor haiku man
who hasn't a vowel left.
Who thinks in kilometers
but sees each drop of rain.
He gets no word on paper.

1977

The Baroque Takeover

For many years now

I have been unable

to eat an unadorned egg.

1977

Poet's Salvation

Hugging wet shady nuns

in the Paris métro

is not my idea

of the road to heaven.

1977

On Remembering Jones Beach

Those ineffectual demi-surges
None could consider waves
Lapped nonetheless about our feet
As we waited for deep horizons
To shatter an orange
        morning.

In the days of skinny hot dogs
Drowning in yellow mustard
Screaming for help to the stale
        white buns
We paraded our half-grown bodies
To the redburned crowd and each
        other.

Strange juices of grownup desires
And immense responsibilities
Damped our own young longings
Just enough to make us wonder
If this summer could really be
        the end.

                              19.I.1978

Wide Horizons

The demarcation gapes open
a line one crosses
only at the risk of loss.

The mind's ambiguities
avail nothing
in making the decision
to plunge or remain comfortable:

Dimitri's abyss beckons.
Squirting of punctured ripened fruit
or sterility of unused flesh
are not the only alternatives
but the only acceptable questions.

1978

I laid the floor . . .

I laid the floor in the kitchen today.
It's now flat and tiled,
And the only thing I've laid in weeks.

I'm so flat and tiled—
Someone's bound to walk on me.

18.II.1978

Sunday on Columbia Road

In the Laundromat

I watched a roach

Walk along the rim

Of a washing machine lid

Pregnant and arrogant

Looking no doubt for water.

I ignored it

Until it walked off with my sock.

Washington, 19.II.78

Windows

Windows should be looked out of

With feelings of sadness or joy.

Windows should not be looked into

Because that means trouble.

18.II.78

Doors

Doors can be walked through

Or closed to shut people out—

One must decide which to do

and when.

19.II.78

Confusion

There are oranges in your eyes
And silvery Winter on your cheeks.

Your delicious tongue an airplane
Dropping ambiguous word bombs
Exploding in my vegetable patch,

Now the shy peas cannot tell themselves
From the ambitious tomatoes.

23.II.78

Nice Times

Spring
You motherfucker!
Unreal time
Out of relation to space and matter

The harsh breeze of nature's rebirth
Tailgates Winter's last blast
As February spins around the
Last cold icy curve
March is thrown off careening

The season of paradox arrives
Sneaking in on rubber soles
To razor-sharp against the fresh new air

A renaissance of carbuncled nightmare
Weighing on the spirit like a giant sea
Monster sucking out the essence of joy
And spitting it out again inky dark
Against the light azure open heavens

Wrenching the balance
Ravaging the sky
Returning to the status quo ante bellum.

February 1978

Quiet Nights

The quiet is palpable
Creeping through the room
Invading every corner of the house
Broken only by my footfalls
As I seek out an involvement
And the sporadic jazz music
Blue music, saxophone music
Slow drag music captivates
But distills not dissipates
The stifling quiet of the night.

19.II.78

Spilled Wine Blues

Chicken-liver paté
Some say
Results in spilled wine
That's fine
But let us consider
Litter
Otherwise found
Unwound
All over the flooring
Adoring
The mouth it missed
Too pissed
And that's the gist.

    of it.

19.II.78

The Heart's Lamb Chops

For Mary Beth

Waking up wall-eyed with desire—
if I tongue-wet your contact lenses
will the ambidextrous stroke of midnight
rip my ear from your mouth?

Will the heron's cry unbalance our lips
or the seagull's swoop penetrate our breasts?
Can we drag an image through the mad night
without its edges being chipped?

If our passports are stamped with orange juice
will they let us in to paradise?
Can the dawn really want to
unwire my brain from your toes?

Can your unknown zip code be as
mystical as my unruly dandruff?
Will we ever learn from our tongues
the locus of moistwarm glee ascending

into the wanton frolic of Brussels sprouts?
Spilled wine makes no beer stains
but barbecue yawps unsettle the oatmeal of life
and the bells of hell toll for the shifty-eyed

phantoms of our movie-crazed mind furniture.
Ambitious sheep want more than to be eaten.

4.II.1978

Runny Noses

Runny noses do not

    a romance break,

nor runny penises

    a romance make

but the flu and VD

    will give you troubles.

                              February 1978

March Musings

Love songs are not written

In the dead of night

During a prelude to a kiss

But only when the smooch

Is a recent memory.

> 2.III.78

Sundays at Home

I see a vision
Of hell opening up
And disgorging
Hieronymus Bosch
Back into the night
20th century darkness.

Will it happen this
Fine sunny cold
March Sunday
Perhaps?

5.III.78

No Photograph

No photograph can contain
Your impetuous naturalness
But without a snapshot
Can I trust memory's magic
To apprehend even scraps
Of your lusty physicality?

Your lightning smile
Will always haunt me.

5.III.1978

Gift Horses

Gift horses

Should not be

Looked in the

Ass end either.

5.III.1978

In the Tombs

In the tombs
The past lies documented
Undead, but not living
Dusty shades of those
Who once acted out their lives
Decided the fates of nations
Played a fool, kissed a lover
Now silent paper and cardboard
In the tombs
Awaiting the eye and pen
Of some historian to give them
Their date with eternity
Or some misdirected poet
Rummaging in gone-by ages
To stumble on and rebirth them
In the tombs
The dead lie and wait
For the living to join them.

Suitland, Maryland, 8.III.1978

Bach: Solo Cello

For Mary Beth

The house filled with round warmth
Tones of crackling wood in winter
New Hampshire brittle cold air
How could the German have known
About wooden snow covered fences
The snapping pines in stoned daylight
Or did the pale brilliant winter sun
Of North America's white intensity
Naturally match the Boche's imagination
In the static wonder of blue boned sky
And the frozen puffs of human breath
Entombed in the infinity of art and life?

13.III.1978

You looked so lovely . . .

You looked so lovely

Today

But I didn't tell you.

Then.

I became depressed.

It must be Spring.

Damn.

14.III.1978

Two Poems in Memory of Frank O'Hara

Sitting on the beach
trying to separate
the wheat from the chaff
in the sand
I thought I saw a diamond
in the plunging surf
but it really was a nubile
California brown surfer
whom I asked the question
but she had already surfed
away to the farther shore
and I returned to the moon.

The snow lies there lying
through its melting funny grayness
telling nice little tales
of warmer days to come.
When the Winter snow lies
the Spring will cut your heart out
before the Summer sews it up again.
The seasons make such scars on us.

March, 1978

Rachel of the Skyscraper

Up where the air fasts
Do you feel light-headed
Hallucinating aeolian roses
And the plunder of Troy?
(Was Helen really worth it?)

Out in the street looking up
At the maze of your fortress
I wonder about plunder myself
For fortresses are to be conquered
(But the guards are armed
And I am no Achilles).

How do you scrape skies?
With your mind arching achingly
Over behind the stars racing
Tracing the curvature of the universe
Around the swoop of your thigh
Flesh finally becomes infinite matter
And voices draw us into sleep.

17.III.1978

The Color of Paradise

For Rachel

Should I fall in love with you
and you with me,
what color would our paradise be
green, blue, orange, mauve?

For all lovers have a paradise
and that place is neither black
which is all colors
simultaneously
nor white
which is no color at all.

The answer is
it seems to me
we'll just have to reinvent the rainbow
      together.

23.III.1978

Fear and Loathing

In the street of the used harlots
walks a stranger with an orange cane
taptaping his way through the refuge
of empty brown eyes and brains
bursting with history's snide laughter.

Slowly he softly steps tiptapping alone
slightly smiling at the weight he carries
lurking in the crevices of his mind.

The rather shabby ladies look at him
askance for they've seen his type before
triptapping orange down their street
weaving through the refuse in their heads.

Love and fear follow him in the street
behind squinting ambiguous eyes until
that neon-lit moment of lucidity:
he leaps twisting high cane flashing
and crashes down naked in the broken glass
in the street of the used harlots.

4.IV.1978

The Farouk Epic

Too gross to fit into a poem
the bloated belly protrudes
sagging down on the flowers
of the sunburst Riviera
blubber crushing young girls'
slender sensuous stalks
until at last
living up to his name
epically indulging
the pig killed himself.

1978

O Yeats!

Everything fell apart
disintegrating
the cracks in the wall
shout the millennium
against the wailing wall
while the dwarfs of terra
thwart in and out of all
our most precious possessions
and the thieves at noon
grapple with the locks
that close off our orange
future filled with stars
dulled by thoughts of
      immortality.

2.IV.1978

Questions

Does your long brown hair
Blow swirling in the blue wind
When you stand slightly arched
In the prow of the sailing ship?

Will I ever again in the morning
Hear you say "Come here, look"
With your mouth full of toothpaste
And see before a dark lowering sky
The crazy angled sun turning
Mundane oak trees into
Shimmering silvery birches?

Does the sunlight warm you
with the same laughter
When you're alone
As when I'm with you?

Will the birds sing again
One day before the sun rises
Or will I not awake again
At your side in that small room
With wintry branches tapping the glass
Warm on a cold January morning
When my heart fills my brain?

1978

On Sitting at a Gas Station

Spinning fragments of thoughts
Firewheel across the darkened sky of the mind—
Echoes of light over the lake's roiled waters.
Where have they come from?
Where are they going?
Broken arcs of lightning
Plunge into the soft dulled flesh
Where we lie half asleep
Wondering if we want to make a deal,
Absorbing the outrageous forked fire
Awaiting the summer and heat
To melt the ice around our hearts
And liberate our blood again.

7.IV.1978

A Metaphysical Justification

Poems can be so thin
to slip through keyholes
and surprise you
the next morning
while brushing your teeth
by creeping over
your toes softly
whispering
to your ankle.

2.IV.1978

The Plain Truth and a True Fact

The jukebox is silent

a generation has lost its voice

and turns to violence.

1978

Dangerous Acts

We bleed each of us in different ways
From different wounds of love.

The embrace of perception chills
Synchronous with its expanding warmth.

We cannot escape the corroding acid
That accompanies the sweet fruit
Of kisses exchanged too hastily.

3.VIII.1978

Dream of an Unknown Beach in Paradise

I awoke and saw the sun between your thighs.
Gazing abstractedly between my own legs
I wondered on what beach we lay
Mild surf sucking away the sand
Beneath my heels and your knees.

A shock of light broke my vision
The sea whispered deafeningly in my ear
Your dark head leaned closer to my lips
Which spoke silently of sailors seadrowning
Behind their salt-brined sunglasses
And wondered on what beach we lay.

I said,
    "Rachel
    shatter the sun
    it is blinding me
    touch me again
    explain the stars"

As we awaited the night to restore our senses
And tell us on what beach we lay.

                                Alexandria, 21.IX.1978

Ecology

Lately the washes of this littoral
love in strange patterns in the morning.
Or has the mind altered the landscape
indefatigably warping the view from the shoreline
of the seclusion of this solitary atoll?

The sea struggles to engorge the beachsand
while the backwash of the harbor surrenders
to the corrosive copulation of water and waste,
    ebb and tide.

September 1978

Goodbye-Hello/Existential Angst

To mind-drift
afloat experience
filtering everything
registering nothing,
receptive to sensation
but without memory,
to be a stone
a grain of sand
without thought,
to be a cloud drifting
porous and beautiful
but insubstantial,
to be oneself
even with a lover,
watching a performance
when nothing comes afterward,
to hear the music
to let it penetrate
but move across its surface
like a needle on a record . . .

This state of being:
shellshocked by life
undigested, blind, lame—
the existence of cripples
their loving broken
awash in the littorals
of the time's trends,
a game played by shadows
in the depth of the night.

Alexandria, 25.X.1978

Paradise Reviewed

The doors are closing—
the gates swing shut
on hungry hinges
as the beggars disappear
from slippery city streets
and the metaphors we used before
have lost their understanding.

The drumbeat of nature
our deaf ears tune out in wax
effigies of history—
no need now to take it seriously.
Our bodies and our minds
race out of syncopation,
no emotional logic bothers us
as we divide sex out of life—
we've given up demanding any mystery.

The earth is moving out of tilt
and we can find no grip.
As lovers we're irrelevant
as humans we've no control.
What is there left for us to do
but . . .

Alexandria
October 1978

Cavafy's Dream

He stood on the beach
where he could show off his body
in his T-shirt and blue denims
careless gold chain slung around his neck
naked feet caressing the sand slowly.

How I hated his slender dark limbs,
those sly damp brown eyes slightly slanted
that shy erotic twist of his lips.
I could almost feel their taste on me.

He chose instead a wealthy hot dog vendor.
That ingrate lacks a sense of decorum.

Alexandria
29.XI.1978

Changes

Spring lay on our shoulders gaily
in our newly felt city on the Potomac.

    (Later we watched the cats' eyes
    grow on the 14th Street Bridge)

When Spring gently bleached into Summer,
I began to feel your thoughts.
The season surrounded us
with Egyptian sun, Bavarian rain.

    (Later we would neglect
    elementary courtesies of
    civilized life)

As Summer edged
across Autumn's threshold
we began to lose
the clarities of intimacy.
Fall's colors faded, and our city
chilled into rage.

    (Later, at a distance, we might reflect
    on ironies, on telephones, and
    history's tiresome habit of cycles)

Winter blew its menace through the balustrade.
I should have recognized a dead season.
A brief respite to southern isles?
April in December—
Winter offered little chance of Spring.

Now we stand on separate balconies
watching the same clear cold sky.

December 1978

Beginnings

But . . . I don't understand . . .
It's not difficult.
But . . .
If you think about it.
Please, I don't . . .
Listen!
Yes . . . ?
There was a struggle . . .
Yes . . . ?
You lost.

25.I.1979

Airports play games . . .

Airports play games with you and disorient time.
Airline tickets are symbols of our inability to fly.
At night scurrying flashing cars
splash the runway darkness with colors
and airplanes seem skeletons of themselves
moving with apparent purpose
across the obscure tarmac.
Loudspeaker voices grate the ears
and are of course indecipherable anyway.
Waiting is easy for those with some place to go.

January 1979

Poem Written in the Cold

We know no vernal equinox here
Vermont Winters know no mercy
No romance here—
just the blasted mountain fastness snow
and the southern isles' longing
for the comfort of the sun
the brown arms of the past
We speed down the slope of our lover's back
leap onto the shadowy thighs
where once pleasure lay
ski fast and smoothly into bliss
grateful for the loss of memory
Snow clogs the eyes and
blocks breath back—
paradise of sorts is won.

21.I.1979

Dylan Thomas Remembered on a Bus in Vermont

Pudgy fingers hold the pen

ignorant of the Super Bowl

whilst his addled brain pours out

incontrovertible images

of timeless urgency

No one must care about all this

as long as I sit here

and remember it all.

21.I.1979

Cul de sac

Mean and ambidextrous fortune

voluptuously mystified

lies upon her sulfurous bed—

an ancient crone dreaming,

crooning a *Klagenlied* in my ear.

Transfixed in terrible awe

I lay fulminating frustration

unable to light the balls of fate.

February 1979

Premonition

(For Lynn-Marie Smith)

Soft wind moves mildly
from the North country,
washed daily in the chancy
fresh breathed
rain of Fortuna
across the stagnant city.

It knows no definition
has no parameters
but passes through memories
a knife in the water
from the distant landscape
where chapped fingers of dawn
nip the flesh like crazed
furry snowblind squirrels
entering the limbo of no weather
here in the trespassed city
of diurnal would-be sin.

February 1979

A Message in the German

For Lynn-Marie

The whispering bells in my ear—
"Eine helle Stimme," they said,
"Sie hat eine helle Stimme"
And I knew it was you.

February 1979

Missed Connections

When you said

What are you doing?

I answered

Brooding.

When you asked

About what?

I replied

It doesn't matter.

I was wrong.

February 1979

"Do you have to leave?"

When you said it
my staggered mind flew briefly
into maddened fragments
crashing about the earth
before reassembling
brooding.
I did not want to.
I did not want to.
But I did
goddammit
I did.

February 1979

Two Early Spring Poems

For Lynn-Marie

Nocturnal jazz music
in the late afternoon—
polished mahogany and
deep dark stout
too soon
after that Aufwiedersehen kiss.
It has been a long time
since the last such afternoon.
Chicken and bread in the park
is nice in the sunshine
but no substitute for
the real thing.

Alexandrian afternoon
pale sun, pale beer
blue harbor waters
guarded by the old cannon.
Only the remembered taxi driver
at the bar
and the chilly Spring day
prove the difference
between reality and
nostalgia.

13.III.1979

Wages of Sin

Examining my penis
one celibate night hour
I thought I felt
the earth reverse its turn

but it was only
the neighbor next door
counting his piasters
unaccountably giggling.

3.IV.1979

Lynn-Marie Traveling

Puerto Rico
voodoo throbs of rolling dice
stab lightning
(Spanish dagger)
into the drumtaut belly
of the illusion
that the cerebral
moaning saxophone tells
the truth

Puerto Rico
exemplar of faith!
sunlit garbage
and careening laughter
spreads its blanket
of soporific artifice
soul salsa and divorce
until the last goat
is bled and sacrificed
obscurely to the gods
and we rest
securely
dead
in Manhattan.

3.IV.1979

Oh distant lady . . .

Oh distant lady
its not you I want to touch
fresh air and roller coasters
is where I want to be
my disasters don't add up to much

No change bulges my pockets
as I jaunt the neighborhood
searching out a pleasantness
harmless melodies of the skin trade

Oh transparent lady
show me the way to the song
you know it's been so long

Come on, come on
it won't take any time at all
and the movies won't do
I need reality to fake the fall

Live performances are the best bet
bet'cha, bet'cha bottom
there's nobody here
but you and me
and I'm not even here
behind the tree

Come on, come on
it won't take any time at all
no time at all
and movies never do
we need reality to fake the fall

1979

Untermeyer's Beddoes Ash

Let me, O Lady, delicately interweave
    my tattoo in among your hair,
let me pursue the morbid extravagance
    of my tenor saxophone
into this ingenious torment, ah,
    this grotesque wormhole creeper
trampling bold fellows indiscriminately,
    open artery demanding satisfaction,
summer feet stuck twixt Christmas ribbon
    convinced the Swiss had short beards
as Shakespeare in his youth, on the stage,
    wormed his way to a dignified but
dramatic macabre and exquisite exit
    astraddle the mauve donkey
five pound notes aflame, the deed is done,
    as the chill insinuated its dry bones
shaking down the silver throat of bawdy
    of the old Cairo crow wailing
screams of wet leather shining.
    Moonshine will not soothe the beast.
A fair mustache and bad teeth do not make
    a poet.

1979

Heavy Wind

It seeps into our souls
the mistral
corroding edges
bringing unease into privacy
but we do not call it that—
too redolent of the romantic
for our cynical sophistication.

Natural proximities disturb us
passion is to be avoided.

The lover sighs
"to whom can I surrender?"

We withdraw and merge with the music
to escape the mistral's disenchantments.
But once caught up in it
no skimming delights will suffice
     again.

June 1979

Ikonology

Iconoclast moves the altar

to the left of the splendor

in the vault's pit

where dust specks float

homeless in the sunlight.

When it rains

monuments

steam from their pores

and laugh heartlessly.

June 1979

Rites

Guitar sailing above the crowd
with a touch of lyricism
to hypnotize the mind
while walking through the street
until she briefly appears
flash of color between the cars
that afterward smile on her lips
expands her mind to include
the sacrifice she has just made.

June 1979

Sun Dance

While the muse rests at noon
the dancers creep off for lunch
to return sated
and lie in the luxurious grass
to rise to the occasion
as an arrow under water
in the fullness of the afternoon.

When the muse's eyelids gently blink
and the world comes into focus
the dancers are ready for the fête
in the brightness of the afternoon.

Slowly they join the thin music
their gestures at first oddly disjointed
pale bodies stark against the green
casting no shadows
the bright sun blinding them
in this winesoaked afternoon.

Save for one hornèd satyr
lurking in the corner of the glade
who does not hum the melodies
sullen staring at the dancers
the stunted creature
bent at the hip
malicious and moving
prepares to violate
the laughing afternoon.

June 1979

At the Pier

We discovered
the water no longer laps
against the piles—
it presses with sexualities.
Glaring into the inlet's depth
elicits only our own image.

There are no remedies
the score will never be even
the bar will not be crossed.

The rocks are no longer
on the shore
but in our glasses.
Sirens no longer sing
their song from the rocks
but from shining motor cars—
we dance on floors of wood.

There are no remedies
the score will never be even
the bar will not be crossed.

Where the fish thrash about
in the hectic dance of life
there's no time for mythology
above the crashing of the drums' eulogy.

The door closes
silence has arrived.
There are no remedies
the score will never be even
the bar will not be crossed.

15.VI.1979

On the Graylight Beach

For Lynn-Marie Smith

Lackadaisical gulls moan
beach dwellers fear rain
which inevitably arrives
when they've set up shop.
The surf drowns laughter
muscles shift tension in forgotten strains
the fog-mist encloses like a damp overcoat
drawing out memories of Brighton.
Bank clerks paddle the ball
back and forth
to their droning women in a frenzy
each dreaming of sun-gorged islands
endlessly awaiting their troubadour
to eternalize them.
In the evening they sit in sunburnt ache
bleeding from the eyes
thinking how happy O how lucky we are
and O darling next year
yes next year . . .
Stately gulls shoot from the mist
cruise along the shore feeding for pleasure
above empty beer tins
slowly rocking in the brief sea breeze.
The sun will reappear
and they have time.

July 1979

The Addy Sea I

The old house broods
looming grey over the beach.
Tides do not withdraw its base
storms merely nick its faded wood.

It holds its echoing past
within for only those who
sign in overnight to know
and never recount when gone.

Summer visitors pass it slowly
allowing it but a corner
of their eyes, faces straight ahead
tingles of fear scratch curiosity.

Murder, some say, or perhaps
some nameless act of revenge
no one seems to know for sure
but something happened there.

On the deck of our rented house
laughter grates imagination
forcing reconsideration—
and we quickly make plans for Winter.

Summer 1979

One Summer at Bethany Beach

Among the rocks and seaweed tide of Bethany
they found a body one stunning morning
and this haven of rest for quiet people
seethed with heat and suspicion—
cigarette ends burned late into the night
discussions chased answers: who could it be?

Music box noises ceased to call
youngsters to the ubiquitous ice cream truck
breast-stretched T-shirts gathered in shaken groups
the Addys twisted uneasily in their graves.
Sacrilege had been committed
breaking the sunflower summer too early.
Investigation drew no lines among inhabitants
natives and visitors alike felt the pressure
pools of guilt formed in least expected places.
The supply of experience diminished as all
claimed absence, lack of knowledge, innocence.

Police insistence on an early solution
took down no vacancy signs in lonely windows.
The question persisted
until the news: male, medium height, Caucasian
about twenty
but nothing further to identify
the lovely seaweedcaged body
dented in the skull.

Summer moves on, kisses return
minds shift to simple pleasures
while the chilled young body lies unclaimed.
The occasional vague official statement
gave little satisfaction to those
who stayed the Summer and wondered
why they had been so discomforted
by such a rash, unstable act.

At Summer's end
with no further statement
they trekked across the bay
home at last
to ponder occasionally over coffee
who that young man was
and why he had been . . .
(they didn't care to say it any more)
during their summer vacation
and by whom.

July 1979

In the Torpedo Factory

For Dean Chamberlin

Watching children play in the park
    is no longer enough.

Arabian music attracts the offbeat
    redwine indelibly splatters these poems

arranged on the improvised table.
    Will this add to their historical value?

The Whores of Babylon never tell
    and my lips are sewn together with wire.

                Alexandria, August 1979

TV

I watched the credits for your name

stars

featured players

technicians.

Finally I saw it

assistant grip

for second unit

but, hell, honey

I love you for yourself

not my image of your

station in life.

August 1979

On Leaving from Red Hook

For Kenneth Faris
In Memoriam

The sky grinned brightly
but not everyone appeared for the departure.
Ancient travelers once enjoyed such leavetaking
boarding their fragile boats.
They gathered now to celebrate one of them
chasing phantoms of old world wisdom,
imagined furies of the literary life.

On board unknown languages lashed their ears
eyes glazed over with joy and apprehension.
With tumultuous stomachs
frenetic young tongues
they raced to a dockside bar
one last vodka all together
one final bout of taut hysteria
disguised as raucous laughter
one last attempt at a perfect haiku
before that Balkan hand yanked the bell
to summon me aboard unvaccinated.

The sky grinned brightly at them
New York City bid no farewells then
but the Captain's whites
nursed occasional brown stains.

Not yet knowing anyone on the ship
a secret smile appeared—we're off!
Casablanca, Tangiers, Central European bistros
(Are there bistros in Central Europe?
Never mind, never mind.)

A plank crashed on the wharf
and everything began to move—
    away.

                              1979

Before the War

Once I made love in a train
>rushing through the Greek night.

Silent, not to wake the neighbors
>we gave our stretched skin

to Europe and the Mediterranean
>careening by outside the window.

She said, "je t'aime" and I "t'amo"
>but this was before the war

when rain fell softly, nights cooled,
>and the sea inspired passion.

>>Alexandria, August 1979

Friday Afternoon

Cobwebs crawl
silver across the window
arrogantly crystallized with sunshine.
Late afternoon:
only blocks away the river absorbs
day's end with austere dignity
ignoring bland couples
parading its blanched green banks.
Occasional laughter strolls by the window
filling the street with the music of youth.
No shadows gnaw at those edges.
If I joined that parade
someone would surely grab my balls
and explanations would have to be made.
Cobwebs and whiskey are safer.
Yet
whose fist might rap twice later on the door
when evening surrounds the house
and the cobwebs disappear in darkness?

1979

The Porch

From this narrow porch
the sky is the Greek's Toledo:
shocking, foreboding.

Curtained windows distain
great chunks of history
done upon this porch.

They did not want to show
how fragments are contained
on such a narrow veranda.

October 1979

The Garden Café

For Bryan Van Sweringen

Painted toenails
distract eyelids

Pre-emptive thoughts of Winter
interrupt the hurly-burly

Orders shouted in an odd jargon
racket against the street noises

Lazy smiles on sunburned faces
evoke nausea and desire to

Rip the laughter from the air
and throttle it under the table

Instead the desire is choked off
behind a tilted coffee cup

After all, this is one's favorite café
they're not easy to find these days

Here one is known, called by name
the waiter always brings the bill

5.X.1979

Autumn Turns to Winter Too Swiftly

While the Technicolor leaves are falling
and the painting screams on your walls
and the spinach reaches up off the plate
to tear at your throat
do you occasionally wonder why?

When you begin to think the answer is
written on the walls of a Times Square toilet
you're beginning to understand.

19.X.1979

Evening Rushes

Across the slope a
dry brown landscape
soaks in the lingering colors
and a scuttling wind mutely
scrapes the leafless plants.

Dark figurines with muffled step
slide down the hillock
gathering near the abandoned well.

Hoarse whispers rake the air.
Impatient phrases crack like shells
as the glade adjusts slowly to the night.

The figurines ceaselessly jostle
flora and each other, gesturing
until silence suddenly
thrusts into the glade
stilling it.

And a cold deadpan voice
softly announces
"Tonight, tonight . . ."

December 1979

Such as We

Wir Eierköpfe, nicht wahr, ich
meine, was wissen wir überhaupt?
—Hans-Manfred Rau, 1962

Pale ire and envy are
all we can summon now.
Too much instant understanding
frail, mistaken.

Reduced to nodding briefly
or smiling with such sympathy.

A word, a phrase or two
or more, confused
enough to elicit the notion
"I can talk to you so easily"
and further well-meant smiles.

Bits of advice, so freely given
of which the sky takes no notice
the chair's springs snap unbidden
footfalls in the flat above
do they too need advice?

I'm on my way . . .

January 1980

An Event

Disordered references
guideposts of ragged lines
heading into nowhere
panther screams of fear and lust
retell stories of heat and light
to enliven chromatic days, shaky nights.

The old woman raises twitching eyelids
mumbling "Watch it, ballbusters,
take heed, cretins, it's coming."

Choked laughter suffocates the idea.

When the red flags flying tornado
finally coldcocks everything in sight
who remains to play Ishmael?

January 1980

Where to Go

No epigrams, please.
    -Bartender at the Edge Bar
        1947

The roads are many, every one
contains a fork or two:
we know which one to take.

Clean breath and teeth
a smile, a grin
eventually the last upon a greasy pillow
or better yet
face down in the flowing gutter
drooling poetry into the waste
that was once a silver life.

The roads are narrow
paved with aging flesh and
mean minds long fallow.

The easiest road's the best
but how to put it to the test?

                New York City
                January 1980

On the Avenue

The avenue erupts unexpectedly
and traffic stops at noon.
Pedestrians' dandruff ceases falling
Macy's bargain basement window empties.
Yawning silent holes in the street
surround the rabid citizens.
Baffled skyscrapers observe the scene
without condoning the event
but do not interfere
though they have a lot to lose.

New York City
January 1980

Love Song

Your lover lies asleep.
You, awake with brandy
ponder lives conjoined if briefly
astonished at hearts that can
no longer feel what they repress.
Leave pen and paper and undress
fall amidst the fragments
of conversations and ideas
scattered in the warm bed.
Drifting brain abandons the thought
that beer and cigarettes will not
tonight give rise to satisfactions
nor the poem this should have been.

Your lover lies restlessly asleep
awaiting perhaps that final leap
you seem so unable to make.
The lamp beside the bed remains
while dulled with sleep you await
the end of the eternal mark
you'd hoped to leave
but left only colored photographs
over which she might laugh or grieve.

Your lover lies asleep alone.
No escape for you this night—or ever
that sleeping form, that trusting figure
for this betrayal you can't atone.
Broken typography will not help
this alcoholic yearning vomit
when culture dies and turning
gray brings no wisdom with it.

January 1980

Song

There are no sea songs for those like us,
the beach is empty, the tide abides,
our best is not enough,
we've learned too much—
for us even the ocean dies
devoured by the sand,
its ancient animus.

Round midnight approaches
but we have lost the music.
Monkish attitudes prevail,
human contact does not avail.
We dwell in our ineptitudes
constructed into attitudes,
sprawling stoned behind Maya's veil.

January 1980

The Last Race

Out of the bushes into the trees
Mad dogs all
Unsurrendering
Spices of life
Sweets of sin
Until we reach safe haven
Land's End of the mind

                        8.II.1980/15.IX.2006

Gypsy Music

Gypsy music does not electrify

but leads to teary smiles

and large tips for the violinist

from guilty emotional minds:

public sobbing is indecent exposure.

February 1980

The Attic

Upstairs in the attic

everything is present,

evidence of your gathered lives

waiting to be remembered—

collected silences

old bones and feathers—

omissions and commissions

by which days are measured.

You climb the stairs

many times a day in the dark.

February 1980

Taken Out

A shotgun blast took him out,
neat, swift, professional,
contract job, clean getaway.

Well, everyone wondered why.
No known gangster connections;
academic degrees, gentle as a hummingbird:
why this blasted death,
so loud, so bloody, so profane?

Jostling memories, glasses in a dining car,
no answer appeared, heads shook slowly,
footsteps moved away from the cortege.

But it was as simple as banal:
he'd abandoned that woman unforgivably.

March 1980

Interregnum

Doors to the funeral pyres remain open
grease-smeared clouds attack the night sky
a hemorrhage of diffused happiness
enigma amidst sad starved rain
traversing the square's mysterious center
where surprised statues quiver in suspense
solid Macintosh savors the deluge.

In the distance the carrousel
begins its rounds
vague music intrigues and lingers
while the mortars thump ever closer.

April 1980

Spanish Night

From the balcony I saw her
stalk off to affront the night—alone.
Sirens in the harbor murmured
to the three-legged dog below.
If she did not return before the sun
I promised to cut my nails
and add them to the terratoma.
Silk scarf around her wrist
she sailed forth to the breakwater;
the yellow dog skid along behind,
talisman for the halt and blind.
Cigarette smoke burned my eyes
and in the squint she disappeared.
It would be noon—or never.
Dusty moorish walls breathe her still.

April 1980

Hochbegabte Schweinerei

Agitated German waiters
Infest my dreams in
Lentil-spotted waistcoats
And small black change bags.
Lothar, you freak,
You tipped them off
For a measly 20 marks
And you've spoiled my dream.

1980/2006

Chicago Layover

The chocolate has melted in my bag
Covering the writing end of my pen.
Scotch tastes weak though I saw it poured.
Another hour to go before the jets roar.
Enough time to wonder what I'm doing here.
Bartender rapping about his absent bookie
      And
I can't remember the phrase that
Would have made a song.
Dammit what am I doing here?
And if I can't think of that line
Then what am I doing here wasting my time
With bombed couples thinking about divorce
And stoned cops dreaming of laws
They cannot enforce?
What am I doing here?
Left my baby in Oklahoma on her way to Texas.
In my new jeans jacket and older cowboy boots
I wonder why I'm drowning in this Greek Metaxas.
A terrible thought now occurs to me:
I'm going to fly that plane all alone!

1980

Empty Suit
or
Paul Newman's Chica OD'd in the South Bronx Streets

Don worry bout heem, Ramon,
He's notheen but a empty suit.

I love you, chico, but your tracks
be leakin on my mattress and
You momma is starvin on a street.

1980

The Wink

Tenpins at midnight
resolve no conundrums
but still we hurl the ball
down the aisle
hoping for release.
The night owl smiles and
shuts one yellow eye.

1980

Lines for Lynn-Marie One Afternoon

I am concentrating like crazy
I have Frank O'Hara's poems
naked and helpless in print
I have Keith Jarrett's solos
reverberating the afternoons
I have my work, my telephone
maps of Provence, guides to Paris
I have the river to walk near
I'll even try walking on the water
but nothing, not even remembrance
can block out your immutable presence
for more than five minutes long
even though I concentrate like crazy.

May 13th, 1980

A Criminal Act

For Nicholas Freeling

Pigeons sneered at him eating pieces
    of bread, not sharing,
his mind back in that small light
    room far down the coast.

Did Judas think Christ a traitor,
    but to what systems?
The police were astounded: what
    d'ya mean went up into the sky?

They interrogated everyone
    but asked the wrong questions.
Pigeons turned their backs in contempt;
    he'd finished the last crumb,
his mind still down the white coast
    in that room where it happened
from which he would never return.

                              1.V.1980

Bethany Beach 1980

Dubious waves scratch the shore
indenting their sentences,
slamming an exclamation point
through seaweed and horseshoe crab shells
making the gesture indifferent to thought.
The shoreline an age old open
wound into which we pour the salve
of ambition and love.
Not Hercules, but Sisyphus is our mentor.
This is no mythology, the water is wet.

May 1980

The Month of May

For Lynn-Marie

You stepped out of the afternoon shower
hair soaked to your cheeks
waterdrops shining on your nipples
and lifted your leg to dry it
foot on the cool bidet rim.
Lying on the bed watching you
in the mirror, I knew
you'd put on the thin white dress
and we'd walk the promenade
and make love after dinner . . .
we were in Spain, in May
and that was why.

Sitges, 29.V.1980

An Imagined Return

The past is not relived or recaptured
returning here after many years;
it is enfolded into the mind and
digested with the present until it
cooks itself into the mind's stewpot
and suddenly recedes into the corner.

Barcelona, 30.V.1980

Saloon

Too many conversations
weather souls and corrode minds
socks tighten
watchbands constrict
one more sip of the swill
infantile warmth develops:
noses run, genitals itch
all's well with the world
home at last:
mindless soporific circle
low threshold satisfaction
speeds through stained glasses . . .
marvelous for poets
disaster for poems.

1980

Captain Harry

Captain Harry the one-armed bandit
whose name meant tomorrow in German
did not have many left.
He never learned to whistle
and hardly made a dime.
She never mentioned whistling
but told him where to put the stump.
What else could a one-armed bandit
do except run a boat in exile?

Bethany, July 1980

The Addy Sea II

The house is warped
but no music plays there
that we can hear;
its joints are out of plumb—
the guests don't seem to care
too busy telling tales to each other.
The sunglasses have changed position
without their owner's permission
while she slept in the night.
At breakfast Jessie said
"I had a strange dream last night."
The demon grinned across the table
"That was no dream, kid" and the
gargoyle chuckled and climbed back.

5.VII.1980

For Ernst Toller in Memoriam

The rules of the game keep changing
    but at twenty-five one keeps up
having seen Renoir in one's youth
    and knowing 1939 was not the end.
Uns versetzen, können wir leider nicht,
    said the poet who must have known:
suicide in a New York City hotel
    no tattoos ravishing his pale skin at 40.
Now a society bears his holy name.
    When there are no rules, terror rules,
but later we commiserate only with shadows.
    "He was a bit of a bastard, wasn't he?"
He'd served his time, gave his youth
    for fatherland and revolution,
never hearing the new freedom of bebop.
    "But we won, goddammit, we won!"
The belt he used to tie up his neck, mind,
    adored museum piece behind glass,
strangled a rebellious epoch forever.
    "Always raising money for something."
One suit, shiny pants, frayed cuffs,
    saw the ass end of how many trains,
unpolished shoes how many meeting halls,
    crying "No pasaran!" into countless nights.
"Well, I gave a bit when I had it."
    And 1939 was the end of something real.

                                              July 1980

An Objective Day

The beach lay back awaiting it rapist,
the sun's scorching revenge
and sandy crotches are its only defenses.
No quarter or mercy would be shown
over the Webber cooking utensils:
everyone would come up short.
Old lovers smile gently at each other
and lovingly finger their razors.
Someone would not make it home that night.
That little town had no rainbow
so it ordered the sky painted blue;
hair-triggered citizens slashed rubbers
and marched barefoot on the tracks out of town
leaving stretches of skin with each step.
There would be no housecleaning
after they wasted the supine beach;
everything would simply fade away
until next year's straw hats waltzed again.

Bethany Beach, 1980

On Awakening

The clutch of dry throat

filled with an unexplained lump

needing bloodymarys to dissolve

greet the morning unsmiling

but with irrational hope for the day

closing off no possibilities but

accepting the clatter of rain

on the tin roof as a portent.

1980

At the Beach

> All I ask of you
> is make
> my wildest dreams
> come true.
>   -Steely Dan

Summer metal hinges on the door corrode
I watch the waves in your sunglasses
my back to the sea filled with sailors.
Twenty-five steps from our screened cottage
our dusty road lies uncovered in July
beyond the clogged confines of city life.
The air turns purple with our sexuality
our minds race ahead of our bodies
but the flesh is rarely disappointed.
We've left deep thoughts behind with winter skin
we revel now in each other's sunheated juices
feeling emotions glide across slippery thighs.

Outside tourists jostle the sunshine indifferently
adding nothing to our happiness but ever present.
Ignoring them we turn again to
devour each other's desires with giddy caresses.

        1980

The Writer in Mississippi

For Moira Egan

When the door opens Autumn leaves enter
swirl around the floor under the table
rustling brown and red
across unmoving scuffed brown shoes
finally crash into the bright fireplace.
The eyes to which the shoes belong
lift slowly from the half-finished page
to seek poetry in the flames
and the label on green bottles.
Compulsion returns his eyes to the sheet
upon which the soul of the land
painfully appears.

August 1980

Variations on a Theme

For Lynn-Marie

Winter arrives
bringing Summer's
promises
in a bag—
but may not
take them out.

Winter bristles
forgetting
Summer's smooth
surface.

Snow falls.
Summer's promise
turns to ice
or melts.

September 1980

Aliens in Paradise

For Peter Clark

Languishing near the waters of Babylon
they await the arrival—little hope
but eyes flashing outrage.
Too long indifferent they now hobble about
ulcerated, ear-snapping, pissing on strange feet,
clubbed fists fill the sky shaking.
Sparse clouds remain indifferent.
Night brings grim dreams, uneasy sleep
on hostile banks of sand still sunwarm.
They will become indifferent to their fate
unless something happens soon.
When it does they will not notice it.
The young shepherdess in angel disguise
moves too easily among the exiles
awaiting transit visas to the other side.
Roll, Jordan, roll.

September 1980

Intimations of Another World

White stars in a white universe

reminders of alien probes

penetrating that smooth tissue,

startling in the Summer months.

The sun cannot hide this evidence:

past violation of youthful flesh.

9/1980

Quest

We are our own archeologists

dressed in morning grey

rummaging in the closed attics

of half-remembered street addresses

absently hoping to stumble, finally,

across a piece of meaning, an old toy

to answer the nagging question of

why we haven't shaved in four days.

9/1980

Harry Lime

How well I remember that Vienna
in that time of shrieking dust,
blackmarket of the soul and nylons
for a meal, a night of dry sex.
Thunderbolts of Mars silenced in rubble,
dull frightened eyes behind war's glaze.
That damned zither in Grinzing
slithered out of the shadows
confronting us with occupation and
strange tongues not heard in years.
But you, Harry, all of you, bastard
scavengers of our ruins, no literature
contains your pasty faces grinning
ashamed, arrogant, quizzical—
you will always be with us, damn you.

29.IX.1980

The Saving Grace

For Erica Jong, Historian

Ah, glorious strumpet,
no more taverns for you,
warm cocknest,
out of the barnyard forever!
Ah, lacy basket bawd,
the streets will no more see you,
beasts drool no more on your knockers,
bluelined alabaster thighs
no more rude abrasions suffer.
Ah, picturesque wanton,
grateful hussy of the lanes,
no more raw gin thy throat set aflame.
To Millberry Gardens, the two of us!
Three hundred quid per annum, enough.
But what the streets, the rakes, have lost,
have I gained?
Ah, magnificent trollop,
wrap your thighs about my ears
and let me bury my dreams.

1980

The Fall

In the realm where animals dream
all things mystify, turn to jelly,
anxiously drifting toward the end.
The small writing table from the corner
somehow is there, too, drifting.
No darkness erodes the light ahead,
the glare is impenetrable.
The figure coasts out over the edge
falling lazily into that bright pool
exquisitely tumbling slowly down,
its screams unheard for hours.

30.X.1980

The Young Professor

"It is," he intones, "the omphalos"
and pauses
as we look away ears redly tingling
to the hard Winter ground cold outside.

No swords flash in this doom
no helmets gleam through the grey fog
but on and on he drones
and pauses
while the circle remains closed.

The Solution

Mean times came on the land,
minds and bellies grumbled and growled
while respected leaders conferred,
sought solutions to fit their thoughts.

Finally they arose as one announcing
"We have found the answer"
and like the barbarians faced with Rome
they began to smash
what they did not understand.

At the Shore

Sunday afternoon collected itself on the promenade
weariness briefly banished along the shoreline.

Laughter absorbed the pale sun and disappeared
across the sand into the devouring seafoam.

Scarcely moving they perambulated in the heat,
bodies objecting to time with bulk and leisure.

The doctors shot the scream to silence with morphine,
but the river continued its journey to the sea.

The young man held out his arm whispering, "burn me."
Sunday afternoon maintained its routine again.

17.XI.1980

March 26

(For Robert Lowell)

The day before a birthday in one's forties
Leaves one aghast at the past's cluttered fullness
And the future's decreasing tabula rasa.
The agitated yawps of one's thirties
      On occasion
Still maintain a presence of sorts;
The rattled leaps of one's twenties
Surely lurk somewhere on the edge of someone's
      Darkening memory.
The light of those immense teenage days
Has gone so perfectly out.
The past is less a nightmare than an escape
To be rationed carefully, like Nembutal.
The future is no longer endless
And the windows have become so much smaller.

                                    1980-81

Manhattan Melody

For Dean

Ragtag, ragbag
full of endchewed pencils
streets full of wall proverbs
pleading "Tristano lives!"

I wander untoward bliss
in Hackensack awash with pity
and brown paper wrappers
but find it impossible to
cross the river without music.

Terror waits above 10th Street.
The past will now commence.

New York City
18.I.1981

The Audience

In the evening
Listless mind unblocked
Waiting to absorb
Unresisting beige sponge
Half-thoughts floating
Ready to take staged words
The leader unleashes
In practical construct
From whimper to shriek
Reason to babble.
Taken.
Action.
Cut and print.

1981

On the Corner of 4th Street & 6th Avenue

Concentration in O'Henry's broken,
the waiting disturbed by
enthusiastic Japanese
young, studious, attractive.

"Did he pay Mario three dollars in change?"
Bartenders are immune to foreign influence.

She dominates the empty room,
all three of us at the bar.
The waiters are agitated with lust
for alien tongues, the subway rumbles.

She talks and talks in her own English
and, for them, lightens the day
with inconsequentialities,
but, oh, what an accent!
as she reads a waiter's thumb.

New York City
13.V.1981

Sin and Redemption

We who've committed the sin of money
often pay with frustrated hearts,
broken bowels and large clothing bills.

    Toiling in the grey world of work
    minor art and artifice suffices,
    horizons diminish visibly,
    exhaustion precludes satisfaction.

No time, we plead in excuse,
attempts at art reduced to scrawled
lines of verse remembering nostalgia,
events and emotions which may have happened

    or perhaps not at all.
    Turn on the music, let us sing!

19.V.1981

The Addy Sea III

The old lady's joints groan
in the raucous electricity of plastic guitars
but two hundred years of history
absorb the dissonance and
the hour the bus leaves for the city
with its sunburned, giggling cargo
she encloses herself once more in mystery.

Brooding grey over the beach
she greets the next morning
stolid grey dignity restored.

They would soon glibly forget and grow old.
With distain she would not remember them.
Nothing would be the same again for them.
For the Addy Sea, nothing would change.

                         Bethany Beach, Delaware
                         July 1981

Morning

Light hovering on the brink of day
pushed by early motor car engines
sound baffled by the house's thickness
birdsongs hesitate before an open window
a dog barks in the back alley.

Before the implications of the day
yawn with greed ready to absorb us
we slightly turn deeper into the warmth
a five minute limit on its heat
as yet unfocused on anything but sleep
morning erection, ache of unpassed water.

Like Cyclops we search through the window
for a hint of climate: rain or shine.
The alarm's music shocks the universe
recently considered possibilities for remaining
dissipate in the struggle with the sheets
which hardly ever win—and we rise up
creaking, stiff, aging fast
hoping the shower and toothpaste
will put us back together again
for one more day at least.

1981

The New Projector

> A fart in a windstorm
> is worth more than a vague idea.
>   -Anonymous 20th Century Poet

Michael said, when drunk in Spain,
"You are a nice piece" or something
to that effect, in Spain long ago
in young days when things were easier.
But nice pieces were abundant then,
as now, if one looked correctly and
geographically.
Some fires do not pale.
Stained fingers caress the pencil
that writes these lines intemperately
at times—dangerous curves turn around
and we are faced with verbs that
will not activate the senses
only flash across a muted mind
unable to differentiate
between the thighs of time and
the nexus of place.
The ice man may not show up on time
but the garbage will always be collected.

                                    1981

The Marriage Season

For Kate and Martin
9.V.1981

Four seasons they say are given us all
Through which we stand and sometimes fall.
We hunger for one of them throughout our lives
Until knowledge stumbles through our eyes.

When the barbarians stormed the gates
We made the decision to become mates
And guard the fortress with our happiness
And dance to wide-eyed music, oh yes.

We'll go where they walk their lobsters warm
No coffee spoons will mar our charm,
Nor the dust of history smear our day
When we stand on the hill over Galway Bay.

The past is behind us though always near,
The wages of friendship remain uniquely dear.
No family bonds are broken here, but of necessity
Stretched to absorb new life and future possibility.

The torrents of Spring flow in our veins,
No Penelope here awaiting the rains,
No Odysseus rolling thunder flashing metal—
For us time enough and Dew and all things lasting.

Before that lonesome shadow chills the wall
And we hear that distant sibilant call,
We'll forge the lightning bent in forest streams,
Reach beyond time and place, and make our dreams.

E pluribus unum

Mean times came on the land,
minds and bellies grumbled and growled
while respected leaders conferred,
sought resolutions to fit their thoughts.

Finally they rose as one announcing
"We will break the poet and the scholar"
and like the barbarians faced with Rome
they began to smash
what they did not understand.

1981

Apocalypse in Barcelona

Ambiguous about what we'd find
freighted with history, too many books read,
we searched the old city in Barcelona
for the shrine to the century's
painter god's youthful excesses.

Lack of language was no barrier,
we knew what we'd come for more or less
in the traditional old city streets
meandering and bent with medieval arthritis.

The discovery's excitement bleached
into horror as I pushed the door open:
cracked leather, oiled steel, greased and
sullen visages slowly focused in chiaroscuro.

Realization penetrated with a scalpel stab,
the foundations of the century's culture trembled,

The Quatro Gats had become a rockers' hangout.

June 1981

The Athens Hilton

(For Aphrodite Papastephanou)

After Crete what better return:
This colossus of urban modernity?
America über alles.
But the view from the bar!
Orange sun behind the Acropolis
Above the Plaka full of folklore shops.
After Knossos, Mallia, Phaestos
What better reentry into actuality,
This international watering hole?
Would Evans or Schliemann stop here?
The eye returns to the Parthenon
Stark stone dark before the sky.
I taste the first potato chip in Greece.
Returns are poignant only when far away.

                        Athens, 16.IX.1981

Delphi

Those stone houses
Hinged to the rocky hillside
Are now overgrown
With transient culture seekers
Ignorant of the centuries
Before in-flight cinema—
They see only dead stone broken by time.

Ruins at Delphi

When it died the splendor fell
But did not leave the world.
It remains lying on its side.
You must bend your neck and mind
To sense the ancient wonder.
Tramped down by plastic sandals,
Abused by foreign tongues with sunglasses
The magic of the prophecy still speaks
In stone and sky.
The omphalos has shifted
From a local to a cosmic folly.
Where is the difference
Between modern random polls
And the oracle's gaseous incoherencies
Interpreted by an old hairy poet?

1981

Cretan Moon

Silver dot in late afternoon Candia
Almost invisible, hanging alone
Gray in the gray firmament
Over the old Turkish fort guarding the harbor.
The rodless fishermen ignore the ancient disk
But know the fortress is Turkish.
On the seawall we talk of customs,
Attempt the necessary tolerance and
Try to see the colored sails blown full
Before returning to the choked city
      And our time.
Later, in Chania harbor behind the ouzo glasses,
We see the same late afternoon moon
Silver gray in a blood orange sky,
But this is after Knossos in September
And we've so much more to think about.

                                                    1.X.1981

Daughter's Lament on Missing Her Bottle

We're just happy, daddy,
Nothing to worry about,
We're just singing like squirrels.
Go back to bed, daddy, my dear.
We're just going to fly to that tree,
You remember that tree
Over the orchard—
We're going to fly over there
From this window, daddy.

October 1981

The New Poet

I am capable,
    He said wistfully.
I am capable,
    Stronger with general emphasis.
I *am* capable,
    Desirous of being so.
I am *capable,*
    With more personality.
I am capable!
    Intensely with angled arm,
    Fingers expressively akimbo,
Of writing my generation's poem!
    Shouting in the wind
    Of his own rhetoric.

                       1981

Reflection at Mid-Point

If the pains and embarrassments of youth
No longer curl my hairs
At least those of age
Have not get straightened them.

1981

Ten Poses

(For Jim Smith in Saint Paul)

I
Wherever we are
We are not really:
Knowledge of place
Is a rushing stream.

II
Presence is absence
When one is there:
There are always other views
We enjoy—provisionally.

III
The leaf, the blossom
Tears the heart relentlessly:
We remain trapped
In the attitude of tomorrow.

IV
Geography establishes our position
But our minds refuse the limits:
We break out *mores*
On the rack of infinite yearning.

V
Restless minds give over
To eventual stability:
The dangers of balance
We refuse to recognize.

VI

Freedom begins with rejection
Of alien limitations of self:
The world is too narrow
Without constrictions.

VII

Places of rest give us quiet
Where we realize our terror:
Quietude evokes business cards
And three-martini lunches.

VIII

Where edifice wrecks
Mythology saves the soul:
Wine lends itself to epiphany
If attitudes are forgotten.

IX

Women and children first
The message of a dying culture:
Save the poets scribbling
Remnants carved in stone.

X

The last piece of music
A bird alone at sunrise:
Verities we surmise when alone
Awarding ourselves a crooked poem.

24.V.1982

For Romy Schneider

How envious I was of that water
Mediterranean blue blushing to caress
Your perfect swelling popo.
No Avignon pope presided with such grace
At table as your nakedness emblazoned us.

On hearing of your impossible death
I will burn my stuffed blue trout
As penance for never ringing your doorbell.

29.V.1982

Music and the Beast

The piece commenced with blue-tinged chords
Strummed on a Spanish guitar
Over which an oboe began to whine
Fluttery complaints against fate
Until a wall of oddly noted brass
Anchored to this world
Only by three baritone saxophones
Snuffed the oboe out
Before turning on the tympani
To make its displeasure clear.

1982

Moving On

Without love we die too soon
    In fragments
Thrown off to the side of the road
Like empty cigarette packets.

                                     1982

Blind Luck

Please lie down
Your hair's on fire—
Tonight we do the moon
After the cats have gone
And the electricity blows out.
The blue wind's gone now—
Strike a match for luck—
The handwriting's on the wall
But in a strange language.

Let's wait for the sun, she said
And I knew it was too late:
The ship had gone with us aboard,
The gigolo shined his alligators
      And
the bartender began to smirk.

No one noticed your burning hair
Or the trumpet's smoking bell.
Scales clouded the fish's eyes
And I saw it in the sky:
Whispered blasphemies no longer rhyme
All the women have steely dans
And Kant has missed his walk
Leaving the world bereft of time.

They never saw your flaming hair
But I did—silently and forever.

1982

In the Garrigue

From the bedroom window
It was difficult
To sense anything
But the sound
Of the mistral.
So she turned over
And let him have his way.
She no longer cared about logic.

1982

Beginning in Provence

We listen to American jazz music
On small reels of tape deep in Provence,
Rhythms changing faster than the sky's colors,
Rapid strides up the scale to dissonance
Canceling the need for language.

But here in the shadow of the Luberon
We need speech to live and eat.
So we climb out of the easy night
Into the white unknown day
To give ourselves to a new language,
The gashed ochre and rock landscape.

Apt, October 1982

On Hearing Monk in Provence

The fire's end shows no mercy
When the mistral blows cold and howls
Through the wall's allowances in the night.

The Félibrige knew no scene like this:
Without our dissonances they smoothed
Their languages in villages and fields;
No urban discontents blocked their path,
Their minds did not freeze in the terror
That pushed Monk over the edge into silence,
But the city's devouring breath ate their
      Traditions.

                              Apt, October 1982

To the Rombauers

That autumn in a rented Provençal house
We debated the taste of poulet under pressure,
Sought the Vittel until I heard a shout:
"Wait! *Joy* scorns the sacrifice of poulet to steam!"
The Rombauers strike again. Otto was right.
Even in the Vaucluse the *Joy* saves this lout
From the ubiquitous time-saving lure.
A chicken in every pot, yes, but to louse
Up our first poulet here is not whereof we
    Dream.

                        Apt, 10.X.1982

First Mistral

The worst in thirty years, they say.
For two days the north wind has
Bent the cypress, broken the sycamore;
Now the rain attacks the autumn Midi,
Gouts of wind-maddened water
Smash to pieces on red-tiled roofs,
Hurl erratically from one to the next,
Eroding out terror-stricken sanity.
Gray darkness absorbs the daylight.

Behind braced and shuttered windows
Nervous fingers scratching dry throats
We huddle waiting for it to pass.
Our minds aching we try not to cringe
At every lash of air ands screech of wood,
Hoping the electricity will stay on
To make coffee in the morning—
 When it comes.

Tavel, November 1982

Winter Sounds

All year, every year, he heard them,
Their sounds contracting his mind.
The seasons pushed each other aside
But their voices gnawed on and on
Eating his silence with an insect buzz
      Until the day
He caressed her neck with a razor blade
      and
Took a Louisville Slugger to the kids.
And sat smiling in the soundless air
      Until the smell
Drove him from the insulated room
Into the street whose frosty din
Pressed him deeper inside himself.

When the police finally found him
He could not speak a word,
But the awesome blue brilliance of his eyes
Told them that he could still hear too well.

                      Avignon-Paris, 30.XII.1982

In the Mistral

Glowing the yellow village walls blood red
The western sun swooped off the rim
Of the gray rock-split vineyard land
And gave the night to the mistral
(immolating the day for the night).
The mistral's cleansing whoosh,
Indifferent to the shades of color
Pulsed on south in the blue twilight
Looking for the sea and North African sands,
Leaving us behind again
Astounded with delight and awe.

1983

Avignon 1983

So much is gone now except in the mind,
Only husks remain to tease the imagination.

Exhaust corrodes the diminished yellowed ramparts.

Echoing with the shuffle of tourist feet
The golden Palais des Papes reaches for heaven
Stripped of everything but history which is
Stuck away in books and museums.

The amputated stump of Pont St. Benezet
Demands a fee to dance on its crumbling arches.

The once holy city chokes to death,
Its legacy squandered:
The stone fortress across the irascible Rhône
Protects only a broken bridge.

The gap between history and the present widens
And no conductor hurls energy across it:
Wisps of private fantasies sound the abyss
But remain incomplete, frustrated.

Now the holy automobile demands severe discipline
And on the Place de l'Horloge's wide expanse
Dirty white youths, blank-eyed and antiquated,
Compete with Africans' trinkets for the tourist
               Dollar.

Chez moi

As the mistral sweeps the sky and hilltops
I gaze distracted at the bent cypress trees,
Coffee in the white cup chills slowly as the sun
Picks out for my eye the red tractor
Weaving through the cropped vineyard—
Pen and paper forgotten for the bright moment
As the idea gradually forms the thought:
The red tractor will be home before I am.

                              Tavel, 7.III.1983

Le sang du poète

We often admired that quicksilver mirror
Into which the poet and his sweater disappeared,
After the war, liberated but cold and hungry,
When everything else disappeared into politics.
What poet survived who did not leap,
Escaping engagement on the other side
Where art not ideology quickens the blood.

24.III.1983

Épisode quotidian chez Mme Moure

The unnamed kitten, too small to
Withstand the mistral's galvanic force
Tumbles joyfully in the wind-torn yard,
Head over paws, wind-blown, happy.

Then the hysterical mutt races in pursuit,
Intentions unclear but threatening;
Micheline plunges into the wind
Muttering dialect Italian curses
Accompanied by Madame's panic cries,

"Finette! Finette! Finette!"
which the screaming dog ignores.

Stooping, Micheline gently cuddles the
    Kitten,
Curses soothing into a form of cooing,
And kicks at the dog leaping at her bulk.

The mistral's chilly whoomp
Leaves the sun its yellow brilliance,
But blows askew the balance of
Olive trees, animals and human beings.

                      Tavel, 3.VIII.1983

Tavel Morning

Baking bread smells friendly
When the heat cracks walnuts softly
Muted by the iron oven door.
Café-au-lait snuggles strong and hearty
In wide-mouthed breakfast bowls
Steaming in the rain-washed air.
We smile silently without knowing why.
Summer's hinges begin to creak
As autumn pushes against the season's door.

24.VIII.1983

At the Edge: The Tune Inn

The Tune Inn's raucous chili
Seasoned with Waylon's whiskey growl
Bites the memory's taste buds
Here among the olive trees and lemons
And the melodic cries of "ça va?"

No one here yells "86 the bum!"
Here where waiters practice the ultimate snub
You become an unperson, Mamie,
Let me tell you they know the tricks!
Desperados all of them, uncouth.
When they rush to ask, "Vous choisi?"
I reach for the aspirin in my bag, let me tell you.

There are no signs here for Burma Shave.

Tavel, October 1983.

High Summer in Provence

The heat bleeds away energy
Flies' bodies clog the typewriter
And the dog has ceased barking.

We batten down the shutters against
The dry unexpected gusts that
Burn the bodies' fragile hairs
While flesh resists the heat with sweat
And brains slowly simmer in pots of bone.

When insects interrupt our reading
We become experts with fly swatters
In air too hot for music and we
Search the dull crushed sky in vain
For traces of the fabled Midi sunlight.

In a lemming rush for ease, progress,
We've bleached the sky with smoke and
    ashes
And love in memory of a sun-flooded south
We came too late to learn or penetrate.
Too much alive to the past, we

Encumber ourselves with nostalgia.
Dependent on churlishly accepted machines
We loudly yearn to adore the clean
    Brilliance
Of this still magnetic landscape as we
Steer the car through the greenbrown
    Garrigue

Thinking too much, complaining too much
While the Cyprus and olive trees rush by us.

                        Nîmes, July 1983

The Fishermen and the Poets

The fishermen and the poets have
Broken their lines so often
Both returning in the evening with empty nets and
    Heads.

They sat too long alone
Waiting for something to bite
Both returning in the evening with empty hands and
    Bellies.

Trying too hard with form
They never found the substance
Both returning in the evening with empty eyes and
    Pockets.

Now the fishermen bring excuses or sneak off to
    The market
The poets bring abandoned words tossed on pieces
    Of paper
Both returning in the evening with empty hands and
    Heads.

                                    Tavel, 18.X.1983

Summation

In the dusk he stares mildly before him.
Under an overlay of fine yellow dust
A summary of life lies on a small table
Awaiting the cataloger's listing hand.

No question of immortality disturbs
The placid puddle of his serene indifference,
But the destination of his artifacts
Uncomfortably activates his shortened memory.

These frail things are the only legacy:
A slim manuscript carefully written in ink,
A cracked Dijon mustard jar holding up pencils,
A copybook journal of one year in Mexico . . .

Everything else ended in the dustbin:
The reduction of life to its purest elements,
Enough, he thinks, to give it true meaning.
The cataloger is due momentarily.

28.XI.1983

Walls

The possibilities of walls stagger me
Comforting and frightening
They know too much to remain bare
We hang our projections on their
Endless promises until we see ourselves
Organized on hooks grandly displayed.
Wiggling will not help here:
It will take dynamite to change this fate.

1983/2006

Last Train Out

We may never meet again
After this last train
Before the war
Breaks apart the social mind
And borders close like vises
On the lungs of refugees.

1984

Memorials

The Auschwitz complex
Left me cold,
All those dusty shoes
And suitcases
And eyeglasses
And faded human hair
        -a shabby museum exhibit.

The sterile building at Majdanek
Left me flat—
The gas chamber
And ovens
Next to the giant memorial mass.

But at Treblinka
Where nothing's left but stone
Stone
Stone
At Treblinka
I lost control
My guts hurt
I looked in vain for solace.
I still want to scream.

Reality is only palatable
In symbols after it's gone.

1984

Three Sisters

At Ravensbrück
After marching from Auschwitz
They tried to register those who made it.

So sick and tired
We wanted to live so much.

We came up to the SS table:
Two seconds to find a new name.
What is more Christian
Than Christine?
Done.

My two sisters could pass with their own.
Now if they only remember
Not to call me Rosalie
Maybe we'll have a better chance.

1984

The Wrong Target

The Warsaw cab driver insisted
All the way to the airport:
American stupidity over Hiroshima,
"You bombed the wrong city.
If you dropped it on Moscow then
We'd have no problem now."
He had lived in California
(no goddamned Russians there) and
regretted his return, and his
West Coast driver's license had expired.
At the shabby terminal
I was glad to get out, glad
to be on to Vienna
where not everyone's a potential cop
and cabbies think less fatal thoughts.

1984

Vincent et Pablo

The old Spaniard
And the doomed Dutchman
Finally sit together
Upright and comfortable
In southern cane chairs
With weak white wine and olives
Enjoying the boules players' ease
Faintly grinning
At the paint-splashers'
Terminal self-portraits of themselves.

December 1984

Washington December

At the hour of tea
(so rarely taken here)
the yellow rainmist hangs
around the street lights
affording a bleak glow
to the sudden chill of a month
unable to decide its season.
The mind can no longer stretch
to conceive of spring or warmth.

                                    1985

Sick Days

Read
Whilst abed
With an empty head
And the flu:
    Scumbler
    Marriage of True Minds
    Djuna
And, as always
    Ellmann's Joyce.

21.X.1985

After the Fog

It lingers like the tingle of a lover's kiss
Or the exhaustion of a recent illness.
It rolls slowly up the back of the neck
Forming a chokehold around the throat
Filling the nostrils with cotton
Rendering thought barren and useless.

1986

The Lost Lady

And so, stuffing her handbag
with French dead letters
Blonde Eileen
moved by a circuitous route
to Corsica
whence she never returned.

1986

Baths and Showers

Baths were not meant to cleanse
But to arouse or relax the taker.
Showers are for cleansing the body—
At least in any rational culture.

1987

Brown Bag

I return home each evening
my brown paper sack neatly folded
emptied of nutrition and taste
like the day spent in the office
from which I return each evening
neatly folded into the subway
emptied of sustenance and joy.

Ca. 1987

Bookshelves Pleasures

If bookshelves groan
It must be with pleasure—
Imagine being weighed down
By beauty and truth.

Letuspray.

Buckled by Joyce and Proust
Testing the strength of your muscles—
What delicious agony.

Strain my tendons, Petrarch,
With all your mental Laura lust.
After all
It's what one carries that counts.

14.XI.1987

Where I Live

In my quarter of the city
When it rains it sometimes
Sparkles on the pavement.
Sometimes the raucous voices
On the street do not disturb.
Sometimes there's a parking space
On the street where I live.
    Etc.

Barring a catastrophe
The market's always open on Saturdays:

Cibola!
        Cibola!
                Cibola!

Memories are short here
A decade is a century
Row after row houses brightly
Colored in suburban finery
Dans mon beau quartier
Indeed.

In the autumn wet leaves stick
To their predestined image and
Lie defeated
Strewn about the street.

                            1987

Cum grano salis

Smashing the dying fly
against the window screen
I put it out of its wisdom.

Ca. 1988

August 1, 1989

The mineral water bottle
Stands three inches from the glass,
Between them rests the bottle cap
On a narrow writing table
In a Warsaw hotel—
Symmetry in the country's chaos.
The mineral water is flat and
The hotel's prices doubled today.

Winter 1989

Dry leaves rustle against the window
Winter wind swift and cold
Drives autumn's remnants down the lane.
Dishwasher sounds muted
Up in the kitchen's annex
While here in the basement
Not even a string quartet
Disturbs the soothing silence.
Nature is all outside
And safety is achieved.

The New Criticism

Samuel Beckett
is the godot
for which
Vladimir and Pozo
wait in vain.

December 1996

On the Death in Paris of Samuel Beckett on December 22, 1989

Oh all to end
Oh end to all
Oh to end all
Oh to all end

Word play
Sounds great
But regret
Came only
In the end
Because all
Had not been
Done.

December 30, 1989

Me and Julie Maigret

Maigret never sat like I do
in a Warsaw hotel
listening to elfish Mozart quartets
transmitted on the radio from the GDR
between certified announcements
celebrating Fräulein Schulze's overfilled weekly quota
But, then, I cannot regularly enjoy
sipping early morning vin blanc
(or Calvados on wintry rainy days)
in drowsy Parisian cafés.

Tant pis for me!

Ca. 1990

Knowledge Hunger

The métro station pulls away from our rocking car.
When we do move, the child wants to know?
Without hesitation the answer comes:
    It's all relative.
Then why are those people moving without walking?
They're gods of the underground in human form.
And thus are children eventually satisfied
    With reason.

                                    Paris, 17.XI.1990

Friendly Fire

Friends often ask me, "Say, Joe,
What makes America get up and go?"
Wide, wide roads and narrow minds
Endless horizons and very straight lines,
That's what makes America its dough.

Ca. 1991

On Visiting the Petrarch Museum At the Fontaine de la Vaucluse

Petrarch, you fool, how openly you sing
In words like roses on the wing
Of that suburban matron, silly dame,
Who bent your heart to play her game
And gave you so little for sharing your fame.

You should have known better.

13.X.1991

The Absolute Point of it All

Around zero
a round zero
circular null
null around a circle
a round null
nullity around zero

27.XII.93

Weekend in Toulouse

Across the street from the shuttered Hôtel Regina
across the square from the gray train station
the old Victoria placidly houses us travelers
where we await the passage of minutes and days.

No vision arises from the traffic's noise and fumes
to relieve the ache and suck of loneliness and waste.

Early Saturday night drunks out on the street
bellow at their own loneliness and ignorance,
Seek their own fascist relief in booze and violence:

See them kick the old woman in the stomach
See them trip the crippled child and stomp his head
See them laugh and vomit on their own feet.

But this is still France, n'est-çe pas
even the vaguest anticipation of even a frugal repas
bridges the unwelcome present to the longed for future—
and one remains in the hotel room with mineral water
listening to the cheap clock's marking robot time
awaiting the inevitable seep of darkness
and the restaurant's careless opening.

23.III.1996

Wretched of the heavens!
Toilers in the shit!
Join hands all together,
raise your eyes and sing!
(Doo dah, doo dah.)

What have you go to lose?
Your socks? Your clocks?
Your mortgages to the banks?
Break all the links of schlock!
(Hey nonny ding dong.)

Johnny Mack Brown Spends a Night in Tunisia

For Kerry in Upper New England

Arab nightmares pierce western sleep
with the thrilling music of pain as
vertiginous with vertigo the cowboys
light out for the simoon desert
while the caliphs stayed on drinkless
to hear the band play on those old tunes
as Eddie said to the gyrating bass player
something about fate and misunderstanding
the trumpet player's cue to the schnorrer
      and the
progressive ladies tempted their new steel bobbins
to see what they could lash together
for their very own range riders in the crystalline sands
when they arrived back at the ranch dry as bones
after a hard day at the notorious cash bar.
Oop bop sh'bam, mullah, and shalom!

                          Washington DC, 19.IV.97

The Future of the Race

If all the ants in Brazil screamed at
the same time, would we hear them?

The tortured road to blasphemous exaltation
twists in manic spirals toward exhaustion

The lamb lies down with the sheep dog
and both fall whimpering into violet dreams

Mene tekel ufarsin, the poet pleads in vain
searching gimlet-eyed for the blind and the lame.

March 31, 1997

Departures

When he left the house the first time
She expected him to soon return
When he left the house the last time
She no longer had the energy to expect anything.

February 1997

An Act of Love

The aging piano's
recalcitrant stained keys
kiss the fingers that
abuse and bang them

Old Man's Day Dreams

To be able to say, sitting here on the chilly terrace of the palazzo beside one of the minor canals, invalid and smelling of age, that the long corridor of life has been filled with many twists, turns, and digressions, and that one has avidly or not followed most of them, would be to say that the long trip has been worthwhile and that one can now die without regret or frustration would be to transcend the sweet darkness of the small canals and calle in the unforgiving Venice Winter without waiting for Spring.

April 13, 1997

Notions of the Young Joyce

The fierce modesty of age
precludes a boisterous non serviam,
but in the quietus of the napping brain
the dreaded negation metastasizes
seeking its liberating expression.

April, 1997

Our Daily Bread

The disturbing thing about humidity:
the baguette becomes deranged.

Never-Never Land

The morning entered the night
like a shy virgin
approaching the marriage bed

Airborne

Transoceanic Scenes from United Flight 911

The stratosphere's ice-captured white bluescape:
long expanses of frozen lake waters
paternally protected by great peaks of softly fallen snow
stretching onto time's eternity and back into the void.
My timebound mind cannot encompass
this cosmic panorama crossing the edge
where no bars contain the immensity
where no human restraints curtail the vision
of that tender universal connection
as we are moved beyond the naturally seen
to the perceived abstractions of the mind's
relentless search for something larger that itself.

Oh how the rocks of tradition
speed us on to that arid grace of the intellect
where memories are our only points of reference/signposts
Flying west is always a wrenching trip
leading to the snow again, freezing the heart
for the eyeless surgeon to carve with a wooden spatula
into the social shape of quotidian comprehension.
And thus we achieve true democracy for all:
a television set in every kitchen of the mind,
an eternity of Lucy and Desi
and all the bongos in Old Havana.

            Somewhere between Paris and Washington
            25.IX.1999

Yoplait Meets Dannon
or
Creative Lit-Crit Unveiled

—Now, you know what's wrong with language?
—Which?
—Ours, of course, this one.
—What?
—Eh?
—What is wrong with the language? Ours. This one.
—Not flexible enough, not sufficiently compressed. We spend too many words on too few ideas. We need compression, conciseness, new codes, shortness of breath requires brief expression. That's clear.
—Wittgenstein.
—Obscure but to the point. We need to curtail, to limit. Find braces.
—Blake.
—Fine for his time, but we're post-joycean, after all. We're even post-modern.
—We may be post-post. Or even post-past.
—Now you're on line.
—Don't know him, but listen, let me explain it.
—Use an example.
—Yes, of course.
—Use "yogart."
—?
—It's simple. What does the word make you think of?
—Yogurt.
—Yes.
—Art.

—Yes.
—Yogart.
—That's it.
—Yogart?
—The whole compressed critical statement made in one word.
—O.
—Surely you see it. Fits exactly what you meant.
—?
—Yogart is comparable to yogurt: light, creamy, few calories, easy to digest, and soon forgotten. The product of the postpaste critic who thinks the real creativity is criticism.
—Wow.

Unemployment Blues

You wander through the steaming city streets
when summer means breathless heat
and filmy mold under your arms
when the notes of summer songs
never get beyond the first wretched bar
    life is short
    art is shorter
unless you have no art, then—
the streets of summer are all so tired
they all end in the cul-de-sac of your mind.

                                          2000

The Indigent

The sun came up
She snapped her gum
He straightened his back
They were ready
          For anything.

(Variant:)

She stretched a long pale arm
Out to the tall greenleaf tree
And cracked her gum

His claw hand savaged his groin
And he pulled his shoulders back
And pumped his breath

They were ready to beat up the day.

                                      August 2000

The Shadow's Message

Who knows where evil lurks?

What a curious spring
False messenger of hope
So awfully traditional
Bright yellow daffodils
Bend before the force of icy winds
Artic air whips about thin tree limbs
Green-spotted with buds
That might eventually blossom
Crocus and forsythia struggle
Against the recalcitrant winter blasts
Refusing to give way to spring.
Those of us with runny noses
And calcified winter joints
Lie behind windows in sweaters
Awaiting the real spring:
Sun and warmth to thaw the brain
And
Still the long yearning for something else
Again.

Washington DC, March 2001

Corfu Nights

The nightingale's song went unheard
As the swifts careened past our window
Circling out over the dark harbor
Then streaming back keening shrilly
Disturbing our restless quest for sleep.

They believed they were omens of good repute
Full with news of a new world out there.

June 2002

On the Afterdeck at Louie's

Vague thoughts of metaphysical
    Streams and deserts
Struggle against the Cuban band
    On the extra-loud speaker
The band wins and my mind
    Somersaults
To the duck confit and the cool
    Beaded glass of pinot grigio.
In the relative silence of the porch
    Far away from the bar
Waves nibble at the ear's chamber
    And the waiter waits patiently
A fine beginning to the summer
    On the southernmost key.

April 2002

Thinking of Durrell in Key West

This is not Sommières
Nor was meant to be
But it may be as close
As I will ever come
      To living there:

Mediterranean temperament
Point de vue caraïbe, tu sais.

The winds of passion blow
Across the floating mangroves
As over the boules court on the
      Vidourle.

We have neither of us come home
But we will have to make do
      For now.

                          20.VIII.2002

The Watchtower

In the watchtower
High above the grass
I watch their frolicking,
The pleasures of their flesh.

The young today have no time
For aging voyeurs speculatively
                    Eying them.

B-Girls on a Roll

Oh they moved,
Yes they did,
Most surely,
And not only forward either,
Nossir,
But backwards and sidewards
And allaroundwards.

Key West Gecko Serenade

(For Dean, who actually
said it to the dwarf.)

Ambling down the street one day
Looking for a body to meet and greet
I met the flattened body on the pavement
Victim of an unthinking shoe
Attached to an unseeing eye
    Because he was just a little guy.

They skitter across the deck of the porch
Hunting those mosquitoes and flies
Stalking ants too big for their mouths
Patient as a wolf waiting for the moon
Tracking up the window after flies
    Because they're just the little guys.

In the Key West postal parking lot
Examining the day's take of junk mail
I saw in the corner of my eye
The small green creature leap off the curb
I didn't see the dwarf behind the car
As I called out, "Get outta there, little guy!

Hey, pal, how do your songs sound
When you're happy and singing
Or are your rites of passage
As savage as the bigger creatures
Who see you only as a meal?
    Because you're just a little guy.

When the tourists stumble out of Faustos
You know they've not been eating matzos
Tromping their way down Duval
They don't stop to see,
They don't hear the squish, but
What the hell, even if they did know
They wouldn't give a damn
    Because, after all, they're only little guys.

But those of us who've been around a while
And know something about the empty life
Know that joy and pain both cut like a knife
Know they'll be there for us, go the final mile
They're a comfort when we need 'em
And a talent show as well
    And we've come to love 'em
    All the little guys
    Oh yes, all the little guys!

Sunrise in Key West

Three sweeping pointed pelicans
Brown against the orange-pink sunrise
Glide along the Rest Beach shore
Across the White Street pier
Gracefully dipping toward the water
Looking for their breakfast
Having dreamed of large fresh fish.

17/IX/2003

Mausoleum for a Dead Writer

It is all there, they say with pride,
Everything is exactly the way he left it,
They say with the conviction of the righteous.
Of course this is not quite the truth:
The buildings have been renovated,
The liquor bottles are filled with water,
The books molt on their shelves . . .
But all of this does not matter,
Not to the lit-tourists tromping in the gardens
Not to the administering bureaucrats
Counting their Yankee greenbacks
Not to the pedants avid for scraps
Of shopping lists and any ephemera.
The truth is—the place is a graveyard
The soul departed forty years ago
And lives now only in the books of type
         Not in the sunny mausoleum
         In San Francisco de Paula.

                  Key West, August 13, 2003

At the Cemetery in Key West

Will the frenetic geckos
so energized with life
Scamper across my stone?
Will those four sun-orange butterflies
Swoop fluttering in unreasonable patterns
Above my tropic memorial marker?

Will the frightened chickens
Hounded by the unleashed conch dog
Race in panic clucking hysterically
Unseeing past my silent grave
Scattering line tree leaves in the coral dust?

All these questions occurred to me this morning
As I walked in the morning heat among the stones
Knowing that when I joined them
I would no longer care about the answers.
But it is pleasant to think about them now.

March 11, 2003

Tropical Afternoon

The steady monotony of tropical rain
Broken sporadically
By a sudden thunder roll
Out to sea
And the flash of bright lightning
Cutting ever so briefly
Through the dismal gray sky—

The steady monotony of the rain
Never ending, eternally present
Can drive one to drink or the piano
When the electricity breaks
And gray crepuscule
Bleeds into the house
And one can no longer read or think.

Frances Street, 2003

The Offering

She offered me a broken pillow
    For my aching head
And I lay down
    To rest my broken head
On her aching pillow
    On the seacoast
Of Bohemia.

October 2003

Rivers of Nostalgia/Oceans of Kitsch

As much as we might like to
We cannot escape our time.
We hunger for the sustenance
Of even the recent past
But reluctantly make do with now.
The fat of the land is rancid
And the hard rain falls on hill and dale.
Herds of disgorged white obesities
Gobble greasy half-cooked meats
Their fat faces shining as they
Push and grab and shout as they
Distribute their sweaty largesse
As they snort and grubble in the
Plastic and rubber goods filled
With shallow monotony
        And strangling boredom.

Rhodes, July 2004

Diversion

Just me, just you
Everybody's in the pickle jar
What else is new?

2004

Love's Poison

Not all beautiful things are toxic
Some are only paralyzing
And do not distort the lame brain.
Rare is the woman beautiful
Who speaks with silvery tongue
Truth and beauty seldom conjoin.

Key West February 2005

Along the Liston, Corfu

We come along the Liston to sit at the small tables
Under the trees on the Esplanade side
Where the young learn rugby with enthusiasm
To clear the day's dust from our throats
And clotted thoughts from our minds
Before the grilled fish and local wine.

The children are already there,
Not many but loud and cheerful
Until one scrapes her knee in a fall and howls
And the world stands still for a second
Until momma or the nanny soothes the hurt
And the girl laughing once more dives into the crowd.

The children never sleep on Corfu
At midnight they practice their craft
At the top of their shrill happy voices
Along the Liston's crowded thoroughfare
While their nannies and parents sit smiling,
Contented, talking oceans of words
In endless waves in the cafés.

The Liston is dense with these children,
Promenading tourists and city dwellers
(the rural peasants remain rural peasants)
Those of us who are none of the above,
But there for serious scholarly intent and food,
Drink our wine and nibble olives before
Retiring for the night to rise anon
Weary but exhilarated to join the seminar,
The great excuse for the nights of food and wine
In the arcade and garden along the Liston

                                              Key West, 11/III/05

The Place to Go

Where, O where
Do little lambs lie?
In the heavens above
Where the blue birds all fly?
Where Jesse James' grave
Is a church without a nave?
Where the outlaws run the town
And the ladies all do frown
But welcome with an open mind
All that money that all does bind?
Where little lamby pambies
Lie down with the coyote's clambies
And none intend to ever try returning.

12/2005

Scrambled Paradise

I've been to a place
Where the train no longer stops
Where the fires of spring burn brightly
And the river as dry as a desert bone.
No one crosses the street at night
And tigers roam the alleys
With heavy tread and glistening teeth
Their sly laughter filled with lemons.

O I've been to that place
Where the taxis ride in circles
And the streetlights are all yellow
Where the gauchos ride in golf carts
And the women are all pregnant in summer.
The tide rolls out but does not return
To the place where everything is safe.

12/2005

In Durrell's Footsteps

(For Emilie Pine, Traveler)

What remains of the quiet solitude
The sounds of the natural world
Undefiled by mass human beast?
Corfu the island remains, but now
Choked with damp, packed masses
Of sunseeking paleskins, unnatural
Creatures of indeterminate genders
Great thirsts and empty heads.

Away! Away! Take off! Get lost!
Stay home! Pollute your own homes.
Turn the taxi around, Spyros,
Take them out of here. Away!

Soliloquy

(For Bryan, who understands such things)

What is the wham bam
In the lake's wide can-can
When the moon screams obscenities
At the sea's magnetic rolls
And the butter has turned rancid
In the dawn's delayed rising?
The acid has run out, of course,
But where's the clutter's edge?

Dranemain, Lackatocha, 2005

Ron Died

Death of a friend
Grieving time
But not forever.

15.VII.06

The Corfu Event

(In memoriam George Seferis)

It is necessary to dive deeply, then return,
For the blessing of the sea to touch you.
The sun's rays perform a kaleidoscope
In pink and green and yellow gold
As you rise again through the blue sea
Happy to be born again in your time.
The sun now warms you on the stones.
You are so much richer now that you
Know there's something larger
      Than you and I
Behind all the things we see and touch.

                           Key West, 17.IX.2006